Mrs. Whaley Entertains

Also by Emily Whaley with William Baldwin
Mrs. Whaley and Her Charleston Garden

Mrs. Whaley Entertains

Advice, Opinions, and 100 Recipes from a Charleston Kitchen

Emily Whaley

IN CONVERSATION WITH

WILLIAM BALDWIN

Algonquin Books of Chapel Hill
1998

Published by
Algonquin Books of Chapel Hill
Post Office Box 2225
Chapel Hill, North Carolina 27515-2225

a division of
Workman Publishing
708 Broadway
New York, New York 10003

Library of Congress Cataloging-in-Publication Data
Whaley, Emily.
Mrs. Whaley entertains : advice, opinions, and 100 recipes from a Charleston
kitchen / Emily Whaley ; in conversation with William Baldwin.

p.   cm.
Includes index.
ISBN 1-56512-200-3
1. Cookery, American—Southern style.   2. Cookery—South Carolina—
Charleston.   3. Whaley, Emily—Homes and haunts—South Carolina—
Charleston.   I. Baldwin, William P.   II. Title.
TX715.2.S68W47   1998
641.5975—dc21   98-24665
CIP

10   9   8   7   6   5

I put this book together for my grandchildren and I want to dedicate it to them:

Ted

Ben

Kershaw

Douglas

Emily

Sinkler

Helen

Contents

⸺◈⸺

Introduction

O GREATLY PARAPHRASE TWAIN'S HUCKLEBERRY FINN, IT'S POSSIBLE that you know of Emily Whaley from a previous book. In this case, *Mrs. Whaley and Her Charleston Garden*. I was her collaborator on that one as well. Off and on for a period of two years I visited with Emily both in Charleston and at her summer home in Flat Rock, North Carolina. We spent hundreds of hours together and I listened while this gardener in her mid-eighties spoke with a passionate joy about flowers, shrubs, and trees. Not only did we tour her Charleston garden countless times, we visited other gardens and we even shopped in nurseries. And when *Mrs. Whaley and Her Charleston Garden* was finally published, she said, "Billy, when we started this you didn't know a violet from a pine tree, and you still don't."

Let me say in my defense that simply isn't true. But it's very close to true. Still, in that two years I had managed to learn a thing or two from Emily Whaley. Not about flowers, maybe, but I learned a great deal about getting through life and enjoying the process of getting through life.

This project, *Mrs. Whaley Entertains,* went a bit quicker. Off and on for a year I would drive into Charleston and visit Emily. She would entertain me with stories for a couple of hours and then serve me a delicious lunch prepared either by herself or her skillful cook, Margaret. And if you're thinking "nice work if you can get it," you're right. But like any other business, the business of compiling has its more difficult moments. In the middle of April (two days ago to be exact), with the entire manuscript proofed and ready to go, I went back to Charleston one final time in hopes of getting an even better concluding essay.

I found Emily in her garden with five women, total strangers from some far distant state. They were just finishing up a tour and she was posing with them for pictures. With good-byes said and us alone, she chuckled and remarked that it was really something, people wanting their pictures taken with her. I laughed and agreed. She led me to a bench in a recessed corner. The garden had never looked better, never looked more crowded with blossoms and leaves, practically none of which I could identify. (An azalea was at my elbow.) I clicked on the tape recorder.

"Oh, cut that off!" she said. "I brought you here to relax."

And you know, I did. In that instant I forgot about publishing deadlines and all the many other discontents and demands of civilization. We sat beneath the limbs of her neighbor's "borrowed" live oak surrounded on all sides only by the demands of April and we spoke at length about absolutely nothing that was relevant to my mission. Then, satisfied that I was in the proper state of mind, Emily took me inside and gave me the notes to a speech she had delivered the week before. Those notes and her brief explanation of them are pretty much the basis for the concluding chapter, "Pilaus," which you'll be coming to eventually.

As for cooking and entertaining, I'm probably not much better off than I was with learning flowers. I certainly enjoy looking at flowers much more now than I once did, and I suppose I do enjoy eating food a bit more than I did a year ago. I'm a bit more of a connoisseur. I've learned that the secret to a good crab soup is cream and lots of fresh crabmeat. I've learned that properly cooked grits have cooked for an hour. I've gained ten pounds and I've learned that there are joys in responsible behavior that far outweigh the burdens entailed, and I've learned that existence is to be celebrated, not lamented.

Now, with the remainder of this space, I'm going to give you a very brief biographical sketch of Emily Whaley. If you're familiar with *Mrs. Whaley and Her Charleston Garden,* you can skip this.

Emily was born in 1911 in the village of Pinopolis, South Carolina. Her father, Dr. Fishburne—"Doc"—delivered her and at that time gave her the teasing nickname of Cheeka. Doc was a truly larger-than-life person, filled with zestful good humor and endless devotion to his family, patients, community, and bird dogs. Emily's mother, Nan, was his equal in every way. Responsible and persevering, always there for the people around her and the redbirds that waited at the steps for her each morning.

After a sheltered and happy upbringing in Pinopolis, Emily was sent off to boarding school in Charleston, where she managed to do very poorly at everything except sports, the piano, and sewing. At twenty-three she married a promising young lawyer, Ben Scott Whaley, and they lived in Washington, D.C., for several years before returning to Charleston and buying a house on historic Church Street.

Emily would have preferred to be living in the country and it was partly to placate her that her husband "gave" her a formal garden in their narrow backyard. In 1940, the landscape architect Loutrel Briggs laid out what would be, over the years, a very successful joint effort—between him and Emily and, in the most recent time, between her and Junior Robinson, her gardener. The garden is visited by thousands each year.

Emily and Ben had three girls, Miss Em, Anne, and Marty, and along with their husbands and children they appear in both books. In fact, the nucleus of the book in your hands was a recipe collection that Emily originally put together for her grandchildren.

And now having said that, I present to you *Mrs. Whaley Entertains*. An apt enough title, for besides her many other talents, each time she opens her mouth or writes a sentence, Emily does just that—entertains.

Mrs. Whaley Entertains

Advice, Opinions

$\mathcal{L}$ights $\mathcal{O}$n
in the $\mathcal{K}$itchen

———◆———

$\mathcal{L}$IGHTS ON IN THE KITCHEN PROBABLY MEANS SOMEONE IS IN THERE BEING productive—the person who has a sixth sense about other people's physical and psychological states of being and what to provide them with to produce energy and efficiency and comfort. She produces sugar treats and knows a lot about the word *festive* and how what is produced in the kitchen adds to festivities. She also knows where the peroxide is and where the scissors and screwdrivers are hiding, what someone's telephone number is and also who needs a nap or a compliment.

Yes, the kitchen is the physical place most likely to produce comfort and refreshment for body and soul. A place to receive a recharge of energy and enthusiasm—and a new direction if need be.

And yes, I suppose some of you younger women (especially those of you working full-time outside the home) are already gnashing your teeth and rending your veils. Well, I can't help it. This is how I truly feel about being in the kitchen—my idealized vision, at least—and it would be the same as a lie not to say so. Still, I certainly don't mean to suggest that careers are somehow bad. All three of my daughters have enjoyed careers. Nor would I bar men from the kitchen. Most of the men in my own family are excellent cooks and I'm sure they're all capable of finding scissors and offering comfort. And it should be equally obvious that marriage is not a prerequisite for good cooking or love and friendship either. In the Southern village where I grew up four-score years ago, a virtual army of maiden cousins and widow neighbors welcomed me into kitchens that were every bit as welcoming as my own.

So listen, no matter what your schedule or situation, you can still find rewards in cooking and even a spiritual strength in the kitchen. I suspect it's something in the air. A calming ether occupies that space.

But there's more involved than ethers. Life is complicated. You have to work hard at it. That should surprise very few. The kitchen is also a place of learning. With the family absent, the room can be a center of quiet and easeful enjoyment; but with them present, the management skills learned in that kitchen are invaluable. And, naturally, the social skills learned and used in the dining room are the same ones that serve in making friends and keeping them. These two, kitchen and dining room, are where we can truly learn life's lessons, and we learn them through trial and error. Sounds easy? Of course it's not.

In 1934, when my husband, Ben Scott Whaley, and I were first married, we left South Carolina and lived in Washington, D.C., where Ben was a clerk for Senator James F. Byrnes. I had my first experience in independent cooking and entertaining in that city. Sixty-four years later, I'm still imagining that I can organize everything—if I really put my mind to it and if I'm not constantly interrupted—so that it will be no trouble at all, at all, at all, so that I can sit serenely on the front porch dressed up like a fiddler's bitch in my beads and earrings and drink several cocktails and then invite everyone in to supper and have it be perfectly delicious, just the right temperature, sitting there in my latest cooking gadget, the one with the good-looking white domed lid. And when uncovered, this creation will look as wondrous as one of my daughter Marty Whaley Adams's paintings and taste like one of my grandson Kershaw LeClercq's glorious concoctions.

Well, every now and then I come close, but I admit I'm still reaching for that perfect meal. It remains an entertaining challenge rather than an accomplishment. But that's all right with me. I keep happy just imagining.

After all, the food, flowers, and festive fixings are simply the stage set for the next scene. Breaking bread together magically brings humans into closer friendship and warmth. It should be a communion that enriches friendships.

But as the song says, "It ain't necessarily so." You do have to dress up that stage with some care, taking into consideration what your talents and interests are and what those of your guests will be.

So here's the basic rule: Choose people you can listen to without getting either very angry or very bored. Yes, that's pretty basic. And as for being bored, I should add that a person can be boring even if he owns a diamond mine in Africa or she is the CEO of Wal-Mart.

On the other hand, you must be careful to distinguish between uninteresting and timid. When I was a young wife in Charleston, one of my favorite people was the wife of a famous newspaper columnist. She was older than me, but each time we met she would sit me down and say, "Now what are you doing?" Oh, that is a rare gift, to make someone feel they do matter.

Just remember, you can cultivate friendships just as you cultivate flowers. I have found over my eighty-seven years that there are about the same percentages of amusing, gifted, humorous, boring, stingy, and malicious people in every social drawer. Life is short. Plant and tend a friendship garden that will grow and flourish. Expect the best of life and yourself.

Now, what follows are stories about cooking and entertaining that I certainly hope will make the points raised here. And after that are one hundred or so of my favorite recipes.

An Electric Stove

ND NOW, HAVING OFFERED YOU ALL THIS WORLDLY-WISE ADVICE, I WILL describe my own first attempt at cooking and entertaining so you will truly understand that great wisdom is earned the hard way—one meal at a time.

As I've said, being newly married in Washington, D.C., was the circumstance of my first such experience. Growing up in Pinopolis, a village in the South Carolina Low Country, I'd had no occasion or opportunity to cook. Women my age usually weren't taught to cook because their mothers before them didn't know how to cook. Oh, yes, since I was born there's been an enormous change in the preparation of food—everything about the way it's cooked and who cooks it. My mother, Nan, didn't know how to boil an egg when she was a bride. Dad married her in the garden at Belvidere Plantation and swept her off in a runaway buggy. Cooking didn't enter in. Teaching her daughters to cook didn't enter in.

Anyway, our cook in Pinopolis, Catherine (we called her Cat), did not really want children or teenagers in her kitchen, hovering around and over the stove, filling up space, having to be either bumped into or walked around. Neither children nor the dogs, which were always with us. All that just added extra time in the kitchen for her.

It wasn't meanness on her part, because she was a wonderful person. Years later at her funeral, I heard one of her church sisters stand up and say that she wanted to witness to the fact and remind all the church brethren and sisters that Catherine had taught them all to LOVE. It was pure self-preservation when she kept us out of the kitchen. She was in that kitchen from seven in the A.M. until eight at night or later, depending on the season of the year. We never came into the house for supper until it was dark. She had time to sit on the back porch or walk home (her house was about five hundred yards up the village road) between preparing and serving meals, but it was a long day and if she did go home there must have been little serenity there, because there were always small children and the quarters weren't large.

When she was sixteen, Catherine came to us as my younger sister Peach's nurse, and when Peach became self-sufficient and independent, Catherine became our cook. Until 1935 or 1936, we were still cooking on a wood-burning stove. In winter it was cozy but in summer it was murderous. To my way of thinking, cooking is an art, but to make a success of this art on a wood-burning stove is truly a feat. Catherine succeeded. She was a marvelous cook. She would have been good at almost anything she undertook because she was quick to understand and absorb and could concentrate for long periods of time. She had acquired self-discipline and self-confidence along the way and I never saw her ruffled or irritable or unable to be effective.

As an example, in those days we had no screens and we had a pack of hounds. The hounds were pretty well trained to stay out of the house, but this particular day Catherine had cooked a leg of lamb. The smell of that roast cooking must have been like a bugle call to action, because Bender, a big black-and-tan dog, the leader of our pack, decided he had to get close to that fragrance.

Catherine had taken the roast out of the oven and put it on a platter on the side of the stove. She knew it would keep warm there while she did the last-minute things that are always needed. She was moving around the kitchen at a fast pace when on one turn she saw Bender disappearing down the back steps, tail in air, roast in mouth. She threw everything down and set off after him. Her adrenaline must have mounted to the sky, because she caught up with him and he was a dog of great determination, as well as personality. Anyhow, his guilt must have overcome him and he dropped the roast. She grabbed it up, lit back to the kitchen, rinsed it off with hot water, put it back on the platter, and entered the dining room as if serenity were the order of the day.

This was the characteristic I would need to emulate, but when I finally married, my knowledge of cooking did not fill a thimble. I knew how to make homemade mayonnaise in a soup plate with a fork, how to cook waffles, custard, and white icing. I had never seen an electric stove.

I do remember thinking that I'd chanced on a piece of valuable wisdom when I fully realized that foods become soft and/or turn brown if exposed to heat. I myself did not have to whistle up the wind, did not have to feel part of things cooking. Cooking took no permission from me to make it so. Cooking simply occurred on its own, doing what people eventually called "its own thing." Cooking was what came naturally when anything was exposed to heat. My only responsibility, I finally caught on, was taking it away from the heat—the stove—before it burned. What a relief this knowledge was!

Now Ben had been living in Washington several years before we were married and amongst his most valued and warm mentors was an older member of his own family, Judge Richard S. Whaley. Judge Whaley was the epitome of the sophisticated, beautifully turned-out, sought-after man-about-town. When he was in his late twenties, he'd been disappointed in love and as a consequence didn't marry for a very long time, but rather became charmed with the independent, well-off life of a bachelor. He was a savvy member of Washington's social scene and had been delighted to take Ben on as his protégé and introduce him into the proper circles. They must have made a bit of a splash when together—both handsome, well turned-out, charming, and fond of making women feel beautiful. But at the same time independent, hard to catch, seeming just a bit out of reach, a challenge with a tiny opening—maybe. (You understand that one of the men I'm describing became my husband!)

When Ben and I married, Dickie (Judge Whaley) was quick to make the transition and gracefully took me on in a very warm and welcoming manner. Dickie had a corner apartment at the Shoreham Hotel—perfect for a bachelor—and he had an unusually nice cook, Carrie, who kept his home and him both in apple-pie order. The first Sunday we were in Washington, he invited us to attend church at St. John's with him and then to join him for midday dinner at his apartment. We were treated to a proper Sunday dinner, ending with the most delicious dessert—Boston cream pie. I'd never tasted this before. A richness that literally melted in my mouth. I also noticed how the judge and Ben were going on over it, and as I'd at least been taught by my mother that "the way to a man's heart is through his stomach," I understood I had to learn how to make that pie.

Having never before been interested in cooking, I'd never thought of asking for a recipe. When I told Dickie and Carrie how utterly delicious the pie was and asked if they would give me the recipe, I found myself treading on thin ice. I do believe both host and cook were shocked. Oh, mercy, that was forward of me. In those days you simply did not ask outright for a special recipe, and after that I knew to approach more guardedly and inquire with a bit more finesse.

Now, having family to cut your teeth on is nice in several ways. Judge Whaley and the young lady who was his favorite companion of the moment were our first dinner guests. Just the four of us, fortunately, and the menu was roasted chicken, rice, vegetables, and cake and ice cream. I had Carrie's sixteen-year-old daughter, Susie, to help with the cooking and serving. To start with, when we were arranging the bar, I asked her please to bring me the liquor from the closet in the bedroom. She stopped for a moment with an undecided expression on her face and finally got out: "Mrs. Emily, they speak of it in social circles in Washington as whiskey." "Oh?" I said. "All right, bring me the whiskey." Actually, it was Dad's moonshine. He'd given us one of his small kegs when we left Pinopolis and Ben had siphoned it off into bottles. Still, it was good to have sixteen-year-old Susie preparing me for the Washington social scene.

As for the meal itself, there in the Washington apartment was the first electric stove I had ever seen in my life. And Susie, who might have known how to cook very well, wasn't ready to correct me for a second time that day. I roasted the chicken.

That night when Susie set the chicken down in front of Ben, she set it down in front of a man who'd never carved anything more than a sandwich in *his* life. But he was an effective person who loved to take charge, so I wasn't the least bit nervous about his ability to carve gracefully. However, this chicken turned out to be a horse of a different color, so to speak. When he put the carving fork into a place that you'd think would be a likely place to start, the fork didn't seem to want to go in. Ben's face showed surprise and then determination. Still, he could not cut the leg off that chicken. He would have had to tear it apart with his hands. By this time the rest of us were aware that all was not as expected with the chicken. So what the hell—we just ate vegetables and dessert. We took it all in stride and I've not thought of it again until today. But I evidently absorbed the lessons, because the vulgar word *liquor* is seldom in my vocabulary and I've served many a chicken since without disaster.

A footnote for the serious cook: I suspect my mistake was putting the chicken in a very hot oven, probably five hundred degrees. I put the chicken in and, of course, it browned beautifully—and quickly. And I thought, Great, this is duck soup. This thing has cooked in just ten minutes. Then, proud as can be, I had presented it to Ben and our guests.

A Black Pot

○━━━●◦●━━━○

I N SOUTH CAROLINA'S LOW COUNTRY, A
CAST-IRON POT WAS A POSSESSION THAT
every family considered a necessity. These were big
black iron pots about eighteen inches in diameter, able to hold
twenty gallons or so, with short legs—legs just long enough to
allow a fire to be built underneath. They were strictly outdoor
pots. All kinds of things boiled or simmered in those pots. On
the sea islands, it might be a bass-head stew. Ben's mother was a
master when it came to bass-head stew. It contained the heads
(no eyes, though—you couldn't be faced with that) and shoulders of the twenty- to sixty-pound sea bass the men used to
adore to fish for off our beaches. Catching them could be an occasion for festivity among friends and neighbors. When the bass
were running in the surf, it was a feast day for all concerned.

Sadly, our pot in Pinopolis was never filled with anything so
glamorous. We missed a chance there, I think. We must have had
many chances for such happy get-togethers. Dad hunted pretty
regularly and we could have had venison or duck stews, chicken
bogs, etc., etc.— but we didn't, I don't know why. Maybe who
to invite was too worrisome, like a wedding list—tough to

know when to stop. Anyhow, our pot was very useful. Every day it was used to cook for the ten to twenty dogs we kept. I never tasted what came out of the pot for the dogs, but if the smells that emanated indicated anything, it was tasty stuff. Often it was ground corn and crackling. Crackling was a dried concoction of leftover odds and ends from butchering and the dogs loved it. Also, we had a similar cast-iron pot that was part of our laundry equipment. We often boiled sheets and blankets and towels and the like, but what I'm about to describe is the emergency use that such a pot could be put to.

You see, Charleston and the area around gets more than its share of storms—plus some. We had Hurricane Hugo a decade ago, which flooded the city, and my garden along with it. Severe, but certainly not the only storm. In 1938, Ben and I had just returned from Washington and were living at 128 Church Street. I heard a sound out on the cobblestone street, at Chalmers and Church. There was a big warehouse on Chalmers where they kept the trucks that delivered beer and the sound I heard was like two trucks racing over those stones. I went to the window and saw the sound was actually a terrible storm, not trucks at all. Things were flying through the air. I said, "Ben, this is dreadful." The windows were open and the downdraft from the chimney was so violent it covered me with soot. I told Ben the best place to be was on the little pair of steps that led downstairs, so we sat there while our chimney came off and fell into the room next to us. That tornado went right over our house and ended at the market, where it killed eighteen of the people selling vegetables there.

I guess my rehearsal for that disaster had been the hurricane of 1916. That was probably the worst to hit us, maybe even worse than Hugo, because the storm entered just to the south of Charleston. Forty miles away in Pinopolis we were caught in the center as it moved inland and north. When hurricanes hit land they are supposed to calm down and dissipate, but this one evidently didn't know the rules. It roared in at nightfall—and what a night we experienced. I was only five but still remember the crashing sounds above the thud of unending deluges of rain on our tin roof.

The house was three stories, with Dad's office and the kitchen in the basement, and we were all in the third-story bedrooms when the storm hit. The house began to rock and Dad decided we had better go to the ground floor, where the walls were brick. My sister, Peach, was a baby in arms. By the light of a lantern—the only light we had—we went down the steps to the hallway underneath our house and Dad and Nan sat close together in two straight chairs with me standing between Dad's knees and Peach sitting in Nan's lap. It was scary, eerie, and creepy there under the house in the dim lantern light. The wail and screech of the wind, the crashing sounds, and the humidity made for an intensely nerve-racking affair. I can remember Dad sitting there and me standing between his knees and Nan holding Peach and that little square of lantern light. All that noise of crashing.

Unless you've been in one of these storms, it's hard to imagine what a nasty experience it is. But as the wise men inscribed on the inquiring king's ring, "And this too shall pass." When daylight came the wind had moderated and we climbed the back steps to see what devastation surrounded us—and indeed there was: Thirty huge mature pines were down and lapped over each other, but the house had escaped damage. It had held, the roof was on. And then the most surprising and delightful sight met our eyes. There walking up our path were two men—Henry Lucas and his houseman—and between them, hung from a stout stick, was a big black pot of hominy. They were going from house to house to every exhausted (and sometimes distraught) family.

At dawn, they'd found some dry wood in an undamaged shed, built up a fire, and cooked hominy. (You know, that's what we call cooked grits.) Then they carried the pot from house to house and everyone dipped out the serving of hominy they would have for breakfast. I'm sure that black pot is still in existence and cared for by the Lucas family. Maybe it sits at one of this generation's back doors. Maybe they're growing herbs in that black iron pot. I hope so.

And now if you're hungry for hominy, see page 107 for my recipe.

A Pinopolis Breakfast

WANT TO TELL YOU, I WOULD BET MY BOTTOM DOLLAR THAT CAT, THE WONDROUS cook we had in Pinopolis, could have been president of a bank. Absolutely focused. She not only learned quickly, she had perfectly tuned taste buds, too.

As I mentioned, she cooked on a wood-burning stove. And unless you have seen somebody cook on such a stove, I'm not sure you're ever going to understand what that involves, the preparations required. For instance, one kind of wood has to be burned for a hot fire, say, when you're cooking biscuits and you want your oven at 425 degrees. The heat makes breads rise quickly. To cook custard, you put in oak and, naturally, the oak has to be seasoned. It has to have been cut and stacked outside, then restacked to let it air out, and then brought into the house. Cat wasn't chopping wood, of course, but she was directing the work and every room in the house had different lengths in its wood box. The dining room fireplace had logs about two and a half feet long. The kitchen stove needed much shorter logs, plus kindling, which was the lightwood for starting fires. The kitchen had the oak I mentioned for hot fires and a second, cooler-burning wood so the fire could be moderated. I'm too far away from the subject today, but that might have been hickory. If Cat wanted a not-so-hot medium fire, she combined the two—not exactly like turning a knob on a stove front.

Now, in our house, until that kitchen-stove fire was lit, there was no hot water. Catherine lived about a half mile away and she would come in at seven o'clock every morning and build up that fire. Then she would take Dad a pitcher of hot water for his shaving. And she always took him a glass of orange juice and a jigger and a half of whatever he was drinking in the way of spirits— which was usually moonshine.

Cat was the most disapproving person of that business you ever saw in your life. She thought it was a disgrace that any man, much less the county doctor, should do this. She carried on. She was such a thundercloud there in the early morning. But Dad swore he couldn't get out of bed before he got "his foot hot with a drink of liquor."

Anyhow, through sheer disapproval, with her thundercloud presence and Women's Christian Temperance Union lectures, Cat finally broke him of that habit and ended moonshine in the morning. As for breakfast itself, before she went upstairs to Dad she would put on the hominy. Should I say "grits"? It's grits when it comes from the mill. It's hominy when it's cooked. When Cat finished, it was definitely hominy, for it cooked one hour. That's still my rule. I don't care what the Quaker box says about five-minute grits. Not fit to eat. Must be one hour.

To make sure the hominy cooked its due, Cat put it on first and then carried Dad his shaving water and drink. After that she would come back and prepare the rest of breakfast, which varied depending on the time of year. Sometimes fried fish. Sometimes venison balls. Sometimes lamb chops—people raised a lot of sheep in our part of the country at that time. These were what Nan called the relishes.

Yes, breakfast was a big meal. After that hominy and relish course, Cat served the most wonderful waffles you ever tasted (and I've given you the recipe on page 113). Dad had his two waffles and his homemade syrup on top of the moonshine, the hominy, and all the rest. Then he was off to work making house calls in the horse and buggy and, unless there was an emergency, hunting one side of the road with his bird dogs on the way out and hunting the other side on the way back. His generation did use hunting to supply their tables. We were raised on game. Venison served in every form—steaks, a roast, a haunch, ground venison, every form you can imagine. (Try the two recipes I've included on pages 184 and 185.) Dad also fished. The fish were always fried. I never remember eating anything so inane as a broiled fish.

Dad and Nan were so active. I mean, when you compare their breakfast to what's eaten today. Can you imagine anybody sitting down to hominy and relish and winding up with two waffles and plenty of butter and syrup—and a pitcher of whole milk on the table? They had three meals a day that size. You would have thought they both would have been square, but they weren't. After that breakfast they filled up their lives.

Meeting Ben

S OME QUALITY OF WARMTH—SOME EN-
CIRCLING ATMOSPHERE—OCCURS WHEN
people sit down together to break bread. There's an in-
timacy that defies exact description, but it's one I've been witness to over and over again in my life. I met my husband, Ben, at
the dinner table. Our family home in Pinopolis was a place of
regular meals at stated hours and an extra place would be set for
anyone who was passing through the village (or anyone else,
grown-up or child, who wanted to join us).

Anyhow, Ben and his senior law partner in Charleston, Tom
Stoney, were passing through Pinopolis at midday. Tom wanted
to talk politics with my father and knew Dad would be in at that
hour. So when they pulled up in our yard, he said, "Ben, stay in
the car and I'll go in and he'll ask me for dinner and I'll say, 'No,
I can't, because I have a young man in the car waiting for me,'
and he will say, 'Tom, bring him in.' Then I'll call you to come
on in." And of course my parents were both exactly that de-
pendable. That's just what ensued—to the letter and for the
better.

While I had no idea I would marry Ben, by the end of the

hour I did suspect I had a new beau. Oh, there's no substitute for the midday meal. That's the time of day when you truly have the warp and woof of life spread before you. And you just might meet your future husband, as I did.

The Virginia Pancake Recipe Story

ARY PORCHER IS, AMONG MUCH ELSE, A NOVELIST. SHE HAS A FAS-cinating personality. She is now one hundred years old, but unfortunately she is in ill health. I still keep up with her. She is my mother's first cousin. My mother's mother was Anne Porcher, one of two children born to Mary Frances, who had come to South Carolina from just outside Richmond, Virginia, and brought the Virginia pancake recipe with her. Mary Frances's other child was my great-uncle Sam.

Mary Frances had a sister who was devoted to her and had married a Mr. Byrd and moved to New York. The two sisters had had a double wedding in Virginia. After Mary Frances's husband, Julius, died during the Civil War in the fighting at Missionary Ridge, she went up to her sister's and at the age of seven, her son, Sam, was sent to boarding school, the Episcopal High School near Washington, D.C., to learn Greek and Latin, among other things. (A cousin of Robert E. Lee, Uncle Sam told us of sitting on the old general's lap.) After boarding school, Sam went to the University of Virginia and eventually became pur-chasing agent for the entire Pennsylvania Railroad. He married

Aunt Maria from Pennsylvania and settled up there in Chestnut Hill. They had three children, including a redheaded boy who contracted tuberculosis and died and my friend Mary. Let me tell you, Mary Porcher was a bombshell.

I don't know many men on this earth who could have managed a daughter like Mary, and Uncle Sam was certainly not one of the few who could. He was very staid and conservative, and she was so vigorous, so tremendously gifted, that when she passed by you, sparks of electricity were in the air. There was nothing Mary wasn't going to try out. Nothing.

But she could focus. She could memorize. She had to decide on an occupation. Would she be a writer or a concert pianist? She ended up writing. She could do anything, but she sucked up the air when she passed by her poor father, my Uncle Sam. He was traditional while Mary was untraditional, back in a time when tradition was still hanging on. I don't know how my Aunt Maria managed.

Finally, when she was thirty-two or thirty-three, Mary married a successful Philadelphia lawyer named Chip Reese, whose wife had tragically died and left him with three beautiful blonde girls, ages eleven, sixteen, and eighteen. And here was Mary, married to a man in his late forties and with a ready-made family. Mary had spent many, many holidays with us in Pinopolis, two weeks at Easter and a week at Thanksgiving usually, and Nan always had Aunt Maria and Uncle Sam to Flat Rock for two weeks each summer. They were all devoted to one another. Anyway,

Mary wanted to do something for me, so when I was nineteen she invited me to join her, along with her husband and children, on a vacation to a ranch in Wyoming. I went to Philadelphia and we all went across the country on a train. This took three days and gave me my first real view of America. I was engaged to Ben at the time. Oh, Mary's girls could sing in parts and do crossword puzzles backwards and forwards and the food on that train was wonderful. And Mary was encouraging me to draw. At the ranch we played bridge and tennis and, of course, each of us had a horse — all of which sticks with me as a most perfect vacation.

Sometime after that Chip Reese died of heart trouble and Mary married James Bond. Oh, I do hate to see Mary getting old — too old, you know. She would write the most scurrilous limericks about all the Republican hopefuls. You should hear what she wrote about Dan "Quaylie," and what she wrote about Bob Dole was outrageous. Anyway, the pancake recipe on page 114 is from her family. It's her mother's.

Oh, yes, and James Bond. When the novelist Ian Fleming began to write his spy thrillers, he named his hero James Bond. I believe President John Kennedy mentioned one of those books as a favorite read and the series just took off. James Bond with his 007 license to kill became a household name. At first, Mary and her husband James Bond thought this was a coincidence, but then in a magazine article Ian Fleming said he'd taken the name off the cover of *Birds of the West Indies*, which Mary's husband had written. Mary wrote him asking if this was true and Fleming confessed that it was. He wrote back that he'd borrowed the name because it sounded masculine but ordinary, in a way that would suit a spy, a name that would blend in. Mary wrote back, "How can you do that?" And Fleming answered that, well, he was sure they could sue him for libel, but to make peace he would let them use the name Ian Fleming any way they wanted. I guess they could have, but they were too good-natured to really care. Or maybe they decided Ian Fleming's name wouldn't do them much good.

Mary Porcher Reese Bond. Oh, she is a pistol. She should have been allowed two lifetimes.

My Wedding

'VE NEVER BEEN A FAN OF BLACK
FRUITCAKE. MY WEDDING CAKE WAS ONE.
Still, I don't like them. Put them in a tin with whiskey
over them and they go on forever. And sooner or later you'll face
fruitcake once too often. They simply never end. But I love a
white fruitcake, particularly one with cherries or the applesauce
one I've included here (see page 207). I make the applesauce
version just before Thanksgiving, then put it in the pantry or on
the counter and have a knife and napkins by for snacking.

The wedding: I was married at eight in the evening in Trinity
Church, the beautiful little Episcopal church in Pinopolis, the
same church where I'd sat beside my mother every Sunday. A
wedding candle was lit and the church had sconces between the
windows. Flowers, of course, everywhere.

This was December 1934, the middle of the Depression, and
I recall my dress cost twenty-two dollars. I had picked a dress for
the bridesmaids that cost sixteen dollars and Nan was very upset
that I had picked something so expensive. She didn't think any of
those bridesmaids could afford sixteen dollars. Can you imagine? But a dollar went a long way back then. The Reverend

Edward Gerry married us. It was his first wedding. Ben and his groomsman Creighton Frampton both claimed Edward was shaking to such a degree that when he had them kneel and prayed over them for a very long time, they got worried. Ben and Creighton were afraid Edward was so rattled that he might accidentally have married them. (Creighton Frampton would end up married to Sally, who became my very good friend and encouraged me to put in a Loutrel Briggs garden. Some time after Ben died, Creighton, long a widower, began to take me out to lunch —a subject that is treated elsewhere.)

Actually, the service itself went very smoothly and the night of that wedding was the loveliest night you ever saw. A high, high sky with the stars going on forever. And all the way back to our house, which was 150 yards or more, Nan had set up low stumps and in the middle of each one was a tin holding a lightwood knot. Every twenty yards she had one of these lit and the smoke just spiraled up through those majestic pine trees and into the blue night sky. All the French doors along the front of the house were open and she had big fires in both the dining room and living room and all that light was spilling out onto the long wide porch.

At each end of the porch she had big bowls filled with punch. To this day I won't serve a punch. You just cannot gauge how strong they are. The alcohol is camouflaged by so many other things. My wedding punch was a light dragoon punch and it was made out of moonshine, the same moonshine Dad kept beneath his bed. I believe the recipe for that punch is in the first Charleston Junior League cookbook—oranges, brandy, etc. I believe the wedding batch might have had a deer head in it. Anyway, the punch had steeped for several days and was waiting in big basins and ice cold.

There were several guests attending who didn't wind up in very good condition. One found himself in the kitchen and kept peering out the door trying to get his bearings. He had imbibed that punch and didn't know what he had drunk. Finally he threw up in the wood box. And one of Ben's special groomsmen, he decided he needed to take one of the bridesmaids (oh, he fell for that girl) out into the garden, out to the arbor. Dad said that a rose arbor with a comfortable bench in it is a very dangerous place for a young girl and he didn't want his garden being used for such, but he needn't have worried that night. This groomsman had taken the prettiest of the bridesmaids out there and in the middle of his tender, loving speech he threw up.

Louisa, who generally tended to matters outside the house, had dressed in a starched outfit to serve. She got tighter and tighter on that punch. I remember her walking through the hall holding up a tray with one hand and calling out, "Fresh fruitcake, have a piece of fresh fruitcake," and then she disappeared into the night.

So that was my wedding. Ben Scott and I had a long, happy life together.

Table Manners

MY MOTHER, NAN, SAW THAT MY EF-
FORTS TO TRAIN MY CHILDREN IN
acceptable table manners were limping and she
decided, with my wholehearted blessing, to see if she could
make a difference. She fully agreed with her sister, my Aunt Em
(who I called Name, since I had been named for her), that it was
important to keep our place as a respectable family. Table manners were an obvious, integral part of being respectable. Our
young family always spent the month of August with her at High
Hills, her summer home in Flat Rock, North Carolina, and it
was there that the opportunity presented itself. She would have a
captive audience on a regular basis.

Nan had often said to me that nothing was ever accomplished in
life without vision, dedication, and perseverance. Well, my vision
was fairly adequate, but as for dedication and perseverance—they
were being undermined by repeated, flagrant failure. My three
girls were more determined to do their own thing, I guess, than I
was determined to change their habits, and my own perseverance
was floating away like the early morning mist before the rising
sun. It was obvious to Nan that these children and their dog-eat-

dog attitude had gotten the best of me. Neither their table manners nor their give-and-take conversation ("She did," "No I didn't," "This is so," "It's not so," "You don't know what you're talking about!!") were going to be a credit to the family.

She felt the tenor of all this needed redirection. None of it was leading down the path we'd expect a respectable family to be following. The girls needed to learn good table manners, the civil give-and-take of ideas, thoughts, and information—interesting conversation. At Flat Rock, Nan was well equipped to undertake the lessons. Her own personality—loving and warm, understanding but firm—fit the task perfectly.

Nan listened to the news on the radio every morning before she got out of bed, so she was always current with whatever was going on nationally and internationally. She had been doing this since I was a little girl growing up in Pinopolis. She was deeply interested in what was happening beyond the boundaries of Pinopolis and High Hills and wanted very much to exchange thoughts with the other grown-ups who were present.

In addition to these assets of curiosity and intellect, she had the asset of household help, which meant she was not trying to cook, clean, educate, and entertain all at the same time. There was nothing distracted about Nan. Her house was in order and everyone, guests included, knew what to expect and reveled in the luxury and serenity of having someone else in charge and everything moving smoothly.

At High Hills, you were awakened at exactly 8:00 A.M. by a

tap on your door. In would come a maid with coffee, tea, hot chocolate, or Ovaltine, depending on what you'd asked for on arrival. You were reminded of this ritual before you went up to bed on the first night of your visit and were also told of the family's morning habits, so that you would feel comfortable and know what to expect.

When the gong rang at nine o'clock, we gathered in the living room for morning prayers. You were expected to be on time and it never even crossed your mind in your wildest dreams to imagine being late. You knew without discussing it that absence or lateness would be unacceptable. When you entered, the ambience of the room was serene, expectant, quiet. Nan would choose a passage from the Bible and I would read it. We would then kneel and she would lead us through several prayers and end with the Lord's Prayer. We would rise from our knees and there would be a general exchange amongst the grown-ups of how they had slept and how they were feeling, and warm solicitations were generously offered where needed.

One of my girls later said to me out of earshot of everyone, "What's this thing with your generation, Mama, always asking each other how they slept and how they feel? Don't grown-up people sleep normally the same way children and teenagers do? And don't they feel fine the way we do, unless they have a head cold? What's all this stuff about Uncle Sam getting a blind headache if he eats corn muffins? And what are all the lamentations from Cousin Deas about orange juice giving her acidity?

What's that? And how can anything that has wheat flour in it disagree with her?"

Well, it was wonderful for everyone that Nan had an experienced cook in the kitchen who had such a memory she not only never consulted a cookbook but could remember who liked what and could eat what. Whenever Uncle Sam and Cousin Deas were there at the same time, she didn't have to be reminded. To the table came corn and wheat muffins, hominy, *and* cream of wheat. Uncle Sam lived above the Mason-Dixon line, where he never had the treat of corn muffins and hominy and hominy bread, and even though the wheat muffins would be there for him, he simply couldn't resist and would sneak a corn muffin here and there when Aunt Maria wasn't watching. And sure enough he would pay the price with a terrible headache and have to remain in his room with the curtains closed.

Anyhow, after prayers Nan would be alerted by the butler that breakfast was ready and we would be invited to go out to our side porch, where breakfast was served. There would be the long blue table set for ten or twelve—fresh flowers in the center, orange juice or melon—looking inviting and expectant, ready and waiting. Our favorite meal set the pervading atmosphere for the day. There were no special places for anyone—guest or not—except for Nan. She would take her seat at the head of the table, tap her glass to get our attention, and say grace. We'd all say "amen" and then she'd ring her little bell and service would begin.

There were always two people serving and someone else in the kitchen cooking all through the meal. *Three people so occupied?* Yes, because what was coming out of the kitchen was so delicious, and it was going down the red lanes of growing children at a steady pace. And this was all before the days of dieting grown-ups, so it was no-holds-barred—sheer enjoyment by everybody.

At High Hills, after the hominy and relishes came the *spécialité de la maison*—sweet thin corn pancakes and honey (the recipe is on page 114). The cook couldn't turn these out fast enough to meet the demand, so at this point a particularly firm hold had to be kept on manners. But all during the meal Nan had her eye on each child's table manners and conversation. She was noticing how they were using their forks and knives, whether they helped themselves to a small amount of everything that was passed to them, whether they used their own knife or the butter knife when the butter was passed, whether they put the honey pitcher back on its saucer or got honey over everything around them, whether there was any jostling with elbows or elbows on the table, and whether there was any snickering at others' expense or any straight-out acrimonious exchanges.

Any infringements on these points resulted in the child's not getting pennies, nickels, or dimes, which were sitting in stacks in full view by Nan's water glass and which could and would be spent by the recipients within the hour, when Nan went for the day's supplies to Mr. Hill's grocery store. No one was excused from the breakfast table before everyone had finished their meal or before those who had passed muster had received their reward. If you hadn't earned enough even for a little stick of chewing gum, it opened your eyes to the unpleasant state of things. Finally, "you may all be excused" did not mean that we scattered helter-skelter. We were expected to follow Nan to the kitchen, where we thanked and praised the cook and serving help for the delicious breakfast.

There Nan picked up the list of needed supplies for the ensuing day, made up for her by the cook, and in ten minutes we would be in the Chevrolet rolling down the driveway headed for Mr. Hill's grocery store. Before we'd be halfway to the main road, we'd be halfway through singing "I've been working on the railroad, all the livelong day," followed by "Camp Town racetrack nine miles long, doo dah, doo dah," followed by "Every time I go to town the boys keep kicking my dog around," and on and on. Our windows would all be down and I know as we passed along we must have sounded like a happy, lively gypsy caravan coming to town.

Once in the store, the children could spend their reward—if they'd earned a reward. Every now and then someone might sneak a nickel over to a culprit when Nan and I weren't looking, but if we saw we would intervene. The first and foremost matter here to be dealt with was acceptable table manners and the basics of civilized give-and-take conversation. I prayed that this goal would soon be accomplished and I very much hoped that at another time soon we'd be able to indulge the joy and pleasures of sharing.

One of Nan's favorite sayings was "Rome was not built in a day." As a young parent, I was just beginning to accept this fact, although I still don't fully understand why you have to tell the same child the same information ten times and it still doesn't seem to mean to them the same thing it means to you, and yet you speak the same language and you are pretty sure the child is not deaf. But thanks to Nan we all survived.

A Flat Rock Breakfast

I DON'T SUPPOSE I SHOULD LEAVE THE SUBJECT OF A FLAT ROCK BREAKFAST without offering you a clearer picture, one not clouded by the bickering of children. Flat Rock, North Carolina, is an old, old summer resort located not too far from the South Carolina border. It's mountainous and cool, a place of steep, winding lanes and houses hidden from each other by dense stands of laurel and white pine.

In the old days, the plantation families living along the coast needed a way to escape the heat and mosquitoes (with their deadly malaria) in the summer. They began with small inland villages like Pinopolis, but eventually many came to make the migration to the mountains each year. My family has had a house in Flat Rock since 1917, a beautiful spot on a large man-made lake. We had horse stalls there, for when they first came, my mother and grandfather both brought horses up by train. The horses would be taken from the boxcars at the foot of the Saluda Grade—the steepest climb, where an extra engine was added. The horses could have fallen the incline was so steep and the going so jerky—so they were ridden and herded the remainder of the way. No paved roads anywhere in the mountains then. Automobiles were a new thing and human passengers went by train up that same long Saluda Grade.

Before building, our family had rented houses. An uncle died and left my grandmother money and she built the house; when I was five or six my mother took it over. As a hostess, Nan set a certain pattern. Everything was the same every year. Everything in the house perfect—sheets ironed, smells lovely. Maids bringing every guest morning coffee. The devotional and then meeting for breakfast. The long bright blue table always set for ten or twelve and only my grandmother and mother keeping the same seats; the rest—guests and children—on the sides. All faced with the most delicious breakfast. Particularly those little corn pancakes that were served nowhere else. They were tiny, about two inches across, very thin, and served with honey.

I never ran across those cakes anyplace else until years and years later. I was in Richmond in a very old club and someone suggested I order the pancakes and oysters and I did. There in Richmond were the same corn cakes. But there they added a thin sliver of Virginia cured ham and on top of that some oysters just frizzled around the edges—with melted butter over the whole thing. I realized then that our corn pancake recipe must have come from my Virginia grandmother, the one who had settled at Belvidere just after the Civil War. Anyway, that Flat Rock house was just the happiest place under my mother's rule. Lovely and relaxing. And I do realize in remembering those times how delightful it was to sit down, a bell by your right hand, and have an uninterrupted meal.

Oh, how I sometimes long to have that little bell by my plate to summon service. Back then I didn't fully, *fully* realize what a wonderful treat it is to be served—uninterrupted—how delightful to savor the flavor, the fragrance, the beauty of artfully cooked and served food. It can be an art form and it is, certainly to me, one of the top basic pleasures of life, one that these days seems confined more and more to restaurant dining.

But the truth is, if I had to change from what I do now, I wouldn't. Getting by on your own is really an entertaining challenge, a creative adventure. Last night, for instance, I took up a new recipe. I don't consider that work. When I myself go to put together the batter for those little Virginia corn cakes, I want them to be the best possible. If today I had to reduce the whole process down to ringing a bell, I wouldn't. I choose the creative end of it as well as the tasty end of it.

There's a challenge to putting something good on the table. Making it right. Like perfecting a game of golf. You don't just go out the first time and hit down the fairway 250 yards. You practice and your score goes down as you perfect the details. The same with a table setting. The same with a table. Nan's blue Flat Rock table served for three inviting meals a day. It didn't take a tremendous amount of money, just a vision and a wish to please. Even today five dollars would paint that table. You add mats and fresh flowers. Making a dress, painting a picture, it's all the same. It's a luxury to be served, but it's an adventure to do for yourself.

Men in the Kitchen

WHEN MY GRANDCHILDREN REACHED THE APPROPRIATE AGE, I OFFERED them each three things. I offered every one of them a wok. I figured a wok could be used for everything from frying fish to making soup to cooking rice. There isn't a damn thing on earth you can't make in a wok. I said, "I'll give you each a wok. And I'll give each of you all the tennis lessons you want and the tennis racket and all the balls you want. And finally I'll give every one of you guitar lessons and a guitar." Well, the last two gifts were successful for some but not for others. The first gift, though, the wok, has been a major success for every single one of them, especially the boys.

I have several grandsons who are comfortable in the kitchen. Perfectly amazing. They started out making fudge (not in the wok). I thought their girlfriends were getting the fudge, but they were eating most of it and carrying the leftovers to the mothers of their girlfriends.

Ted, the oldest, loves to eat. (They all do.) He learned very early on to make a picture-book omelet, with all kinds of sausages tucked in there. Oh, my law, you never saw such attention to detail as he gives that recipe and in the end he has something beautiful enough to be photographed for *Southern Living*. In fact, he does most of the cooking around his house.

My second grandson, Ben, has finished law school and has returned to Charleston. He cooks with the wok probably the most. Spinach is his specialty. Canned, cooked, raw—he eats spinach like Popeye. Ben is the only one who worries about the proper foods. When preparing spinach, he takes out the tough pieces, washes but doesn't shake it, and then straight into a pot that's been sprayed with Pam. Put the cover on and as soon as it's wilted it's ready to eat. That's Ben LeClercq's spinach. And by the way, he also mastered the guitar.

Anne and Fred's youngest, Kershaw, beats his mother to *Gourmet* magazine every month. He picks out the most extravagant and scrumptious recipe in there, goes shopping for the ingredients, and cooks it before nightfall. If his mother has a party, he will cook a couple of desserts for her. He made three lemon pies last Christmas. His meringue is professional.

When Kershaw was nine or so he said, "Cheeka, I want to take you out to dinner." This was just following my husband Ben's death. He said, "I've got the money." Well, I do like to go out to dinner, so I said I'd love to go. "Where are we going?" He said, "I'd like to take you down there to that restaurant on King Street that has all those chickens turning in the window." So we got in the car and went down to this old Greek restaurant. He got me seated and said, "Now I'm ordering the wine, and being as I know what is best here, I'm ordering for you, too." Ben and I had driven by this restaurant for years just to look at the chickens all golden brown and turning slowly in the window, but we had never stopped and gone in. So in the end my nine-year-old grandson took me and we had a perfectly delightful time.

Douglas has treated me like royalty as well. (They all do.) Douglas is the artist. Last year in the mountains he said, "Cheeka, I'd like to cook dinner for you tonight." I said I'd love it. I retired to the front porch with a scotch and soda and paid no attention to the kitchen because I knew that was what he wanted. After a while he announced that dinner was served. He had set the table and lit the candles and he served me a dinner that could have been cooked by a top chef. From soup to nuts.

Anyhow, my grandsons moved into the kitchen and loved what they found there. Fred is the father of Ted, Ben, and Kershaw and he is fun to cook for (an excellent attribute in a man). He's not so much a cook himself, but he enjoys food and will hang over you while it's being prepared. And best of all, when dinner is over he will retire to the kitchen saying, "This is my gift to the evening." And he'll clean up. Absolutely everything. Leaves the kitchen sparkling.

Yes, the basket has been filled with the men in my family.

The Corner Groceries

HE MARKET, THAT LONG BRICK SHED STRETCHING THE THREE BLOCKS BE-tween Meeting Street and East Bay, was still operating as a produce market when we moved back to Charleston in 1938. They also had a meat market in there and vultures really did hover around, waiting to eat the scraps. I didn't buy my meat there. Fortunately I had a fine little grocery straight across the street from our house, the corner of Chalmers and Church. There were corner groceries all over the lower peninsula of Charleston then. It was like having a pantry just outside the front door. When Ben and I lived up the block here on Church, we just switched over to Mr. Hill, who was practically across the street.

For truly fancy items we had Ohlandt at the corner of Water and Meeting (all this purely residential now). When my Aunt Cad would come down here from Philadelphia, she'd always stay at the Villa Margherita and the first thing she'd do was walk around the corner to Ohlandt and pick out big boxes of delica-cies to send to her friends. Smoked oysters, olives, and caviar. True delicacies. Ohlandt was a meeting place for ladies in the morning. I can see them now, the matrons, in their white gloves and their hats. I didn't appreciate that sight at the time, of course. Something so absolutely "Charleston." Later in the morning, the deliveries would be made from a van pulled by a horse. Mind you, this was in 1938.

A block down was Mr. Pete's grocery, but really his main business was fighting gamecocks somewhere in the recesses of that store. I could hear those roosters crowing as the sun came up each morning. I heard them even before St. Michael's bells' ringing or the shrimp man's calling.

Things change. Now we have refrigerators and all manner of freeze-drying. But I can still count on Mr. Burbage. He's a Charleston institution. His store is on the corner of Savage and Broad. He used to deliver but doesn't anymore. On Saturday mornings the children's bicycles will be there. They're spending their week's candy money. Mr. Burbage is adorable with children. He knows everybody by name. He has candy displayed where the children can get at it. The children are just drooling when they come in the door with their nickels and dimes. Each child is introduced to Mr. Burbage by the age of one week and for the rest of their childhoods he oversees their candy intake. One day he says, "Mrs. Whaley, so-and-so is eating an awful lot of candy"—warning me about one of my grandchildren. Mr. Burbage is in his seventies now. His son Al is in business with him. They've changed their format a bit. Al makes delicious things himself. They've always had the best sausages within driving distance. Three different tastes: mild, medium, and hot. Wonderful cuts of meat. Specialties. Soups, broccoli, muffins, homemade rolls, etc. and etc. And Al always keeps my favorite treats—biscotti and lemon sorbet.

Mr. Burbage is from Berkeley County originally, the same as me. His is the last of the old corner groceries in Charleston and maybe the last place you can get true neighborly advice. Just last week he said to me, "If you're afraid you've kept your crabmeat too long, just test it by putting a tiny taste on the tip of your tongue." You should have seen his face as he told me this. His features got all contorted. It seems that sometimes the bad can even feel slimy.

My cook, Margaret, thinks Mr. Burbage hung the moon and stars, and most of the other Charleston cooks agree. I was in there one morning when he was on the phone with a Charleston lady, who was then in her eighties and still playing eighteen holes of golf twice a week. Even so, her mind wasn't especially taken up with variety at dinnertime. She was dictating quite a list to Mr. Burbage, which ended with pork chops. Mr. Burbage wrote it all down and then asked her if he could speak to her cook for a minute. Evidently, her cook was put on and I heard him say, "You know you all had pork chops yesterday for dinner. You should have some chicken or something else today."

So we still have that five-hundred-square-foot pantry in downtown Charleston, and to stop by there in the morning will keep your pulse beating smoothly for the rest of the day.

Poultry

WELL, IT'S ALL TYSON CHICKEN BREASTS TODAY, AND I DO BUY THEM. They come neatly wrapped in clear plastic and are waiting in a refrigerated case in the aisle of a supermarket that's been professionally decorated and scrubbed as clean as a hospital. Thank God. When I was a girl growing up in Pinopolis, you would just pick out one of the chickens running around the yard. I don't want to think about it too much or I'll become a "vegetanarian."

On countless occasions, Dad would call my mother from his office in Moncks Corner and say, "Nancy, Dr. Renken or so-and-so is here. I'm going to bring him for lunch." And Nan would go and call down into the backyard to one of the help: "Louisa, woo-hoo! Louisa! Run a chicken down. Dr. Renken is coming to lunch."

One time we thought my middle daughter, Anne, had swallowed the mercury in a thermometer. She bit the thermometer. Nan tried to stick her finger down her throat, but that child's throat was cemented shut. Nan says, "Run quick! Go to the window and call Louisa to run a chicken down and bring a feather here." We heard more damn squawking and here comes Louisa flying up the steps as though she were carrying the Holy Grail. A chicken feather. Nan had no chance of getting that down Anne's throat either, but it turned out she hadn't swallowed the mercury. She's still alive today and wouldn't be if that had been the case.

While I'm on the subject, I should admit that I can't fry chicken and don't even try. My cook, Margaret, fries it marvelously. When my grandson Ben comes home he wants Margaret's fried chicken and Margaret's mashed potatoes. I mean we all set in. It is the most tender, moist, cooked-to-the bone crisp wonderful treat. But old-time cooks like Margaret are getting rarer and rarer and I don't have her but twice a week now.

There used to be two places we could get good fried chicken in town, but one unfortunately has closed. That's the five-and-ten-cent store, Woolworth's. Best fried chicken in town. The other place is the uptown Piggly Wiggly. And I'll admit that old recipe from Colonel Sanders is very good. When you need fried chicken in big quantities, that's the time to go out for it, when you're having fifteen or twenty people over and you want to eat fried chicken before a football game.

I've mentioned chickens, so I'll include ducks here for good measure. I'm simply not a fan of wild duck—or wild anything else—these days. For one thing, there's less and less game around and hunting is becoming an anachronism. And for another, let me tell you, a wild turkey is not a gourmet delight. Period! And a duck that has flown the Atlantic flyway a couple of times, dodging shot and eating muddy grass, simply does not appeal to me either. But here's a story about cooking duck, so you will see that I am still open-minded on the subject.

We were house-partying down at Yemassee with a very stylish couple, and my husband, Ben, was sitting next to his hostess. Now, there is a fetish with some men, everything must be rare, and our hostess understood that everybody wanted their duck cooked differently. When she comes to me I say, "I want my duck well done." And Ben says, "I want mine to have seen the fire." He meant he wanted the duck to know that it had been in the oven. Instead, they just passed his duck *through* the oven. Here was Ben sitting next to our hostess, and me looking on with the greatest pleasure as he struggled with that perfectly raw duck. Payback. I've had more restaurant meals ruined by men complaining about their steaks not being rare enough—no matter how it comes, it's not rare enough. So I watched Ben with the greatest pleasure trying to eat a duck that had "seen the fire." He stuck his fork in it and it squirted blood. Served him right.

Turtles, Terrapins, and Cooters

ERRAPINS ARE CALLED COOTERS OUT IN THE COUNTRY. AND THEY'RE CALLED cooters in Charleston. As in "cooter soup." *Terrapin* is definitely a word from off. Nobody would have known what you were talking about if you said "terrapin."

For doctoring, Dad received everything in payment. Venison, collards, even cords of wood—stove wood. Dad's father, Mr. Fishburne, was a lawyer in Walterboro and his clients brought him cooters on a regular basis. Cooters were a form of currency. My friend Bettina's great-grandfather was the first of the planters to come down from the upper neighborhood of the Santee River, up above Pinopolis. When they moved to Charleston, food supplies would be delivered from the plantation every week and the supplies would always include a barrel of cooters, which would be let loose in the backyard. Bettina remembers when she was a child watching the yardman chasing cooters around with a hatchet to cut their heads off.

Those were freshwater turtles, but I believe the ones that were sold commercially were saltwater. Anyhow, it's all cooters to me and I'm not particularly anxious to eat one, and certainly not to clean and cook one. Back in the early fifties, Ben went fishing with the old mayor Bill Morrison for spot-tail bass and they picked up a cooter and a big conch. Ben telephones me from somewhere and he says, "We're dividing this up. Do you want the cooter or the big conch?" I say, "Neither one and especially you are not bringing a cooter into my kitchen. You can believe that. Let Bill take the cooter home." Well, Bill was afraid his wife, Caroline, didn't want it in her kitchen either. I say, "You figure somebody who knows how to cook cooters and would appreciate a cooter and give it to them. And don't bring the conch home either! I'll take the shrimp that are left over from the bait, but do not bring the conch or the cooter." I say, "Try Colonel Barnwell. He has a cook that will do it."

So Ben gets around to Colonel Barnwell, but it turns out his cook is sick. He calls me again and I tell him to try Aunt Julia. He says, "First, I'm going to take it by Mr. Moultrie Ball's." Mr. Moultrie Ball says no way. He says, "My cook doesn't know anything about that." So Ben takes it to Aunt Julia. She was born and raised on a plantation on the Cooper River and I thought she would know what to do with it. And she did and they said they'd love it. And Ben comes home without cooters or conchs.

About a week later I ran into Jack Walker, Aunt Julia's son-in-law. I said, "How was the cooter soup?" And he said, "Oh, that cooter." He said, "I took that cooter and threw it over the high battery." So the cooter went back in the harbor, which as far as I'm concerned is where it should have stayed.

Three O'Clock Dinner

THE THREE O'CLOCK DINNER WAS AN OLD CHARLESTON INSTITUTION—THE main meal of the day, served in the midafternoon. In the 1930s, Josephine Pinckney wrote a very popular Charleston novel called *Three O'Clock Dinner*. But you know, by the time people get around to writing about things they are often fading. (The book in your hands being the exception, of course.) And by the thirties, the three o'clock dinner was almost gone. Still, Ben and I enjoyed a slightly adjusted version of it. We ate at two.

Our schedule went thus: Ben was always at work by eight in the morning, but before leaving he and I did something that was very satisfactory. It is difficult to confer about your children if those children are in the house listening. You can't have a conversation that isn't overheard. So Ben and I would get into his automobile at quarter to eight every single morning and we'd drive around the Battery. For one thing, we really did want to see what the weather was going to be, and both being from the country, we felt the only way to know was to be outside looking at it. At the same time, some very important conferring went on. What did he think of this or that? What would he do if this situation turned up? He would counsel me in a very uninterrupted, lawyerly fashion. I suppose it did look perfectly ridiculous. People said they could set their clocks by us as we drove around the Battery discussing what to do about the children.

Then, at dinner, we would attempt to practice what we'd talked over. The girls went to Charleston Day School and got out at ten of two. If you hadn't paid attention in class, you went back at three to be tutored, and at least one of ours was always going back. Anyway, at two, here would come the children, a bicycle parade coming down Church Street. I have a picture of that, all those children coming. One neighbor used to complain furiously, because the children made no bones about coming along the wrong way on Tradd Street and he'd be in his car trying to make his way home. Here would come this mass of bicycling children straight at him. Nowadays, of course, the sad complaint is that the neighborhood structure of these same streets is breaking down and there are many fewer children living here, but I don't think that's so.

Anyway, our girls were home by two and so was Ben, him at one end of the table and me at the other end. My niece Moonee was living with us during her last four years of school, so at that time there were four girls who never missed that two o'clock dinner. And I never missed a dinner either—declined all luncheon invitations as long as the girls were at home.

We had meat, rice and gravy, two vegetables, a salad, and a dessert every single solitary day. Just as regular as the sun came up, that was what was on the table each midday. You know, one of the terrible losses to America is the loss of the midday dinner with adults at each end of the table. That was the way I had been raised. Here, at least, you could hope to continue instilling some sense of moderation and teach the child how to put food in her mouth in a civil fashion. (Yes, I have already confessed that Ben and I had help from Nan in starting this endeavor, but we did manage to persevere and it did finally take hold.) So I never missed a two o'clock dinner, not just because I felt duty-bound, but because that meal was so entertaining. I would hear everything those girls had done that morning, and Ben would hear, too. And they would hear us discuss politics and what Ben and I had each done and at least some concerns of the adult world. And finally, the whole meal did have a happy, relaxed, humorous air to it.

Of course, that was when we had a cook coming five days a week. It seems that when cooks were becoming a thing of the past, the food in America was changing. Perhaps this was a coincidence. In Charleston, at least, the old-time cooks didn't want to make a change. They were marvelous with fried chicken, red rice, all that. The way vegetables are cooked now isn't something the old cooks would change to.

When school lunches were adopted, the children didn't come home anymore, which was sad. The beauty of the two or three o'clock meal was that nobody was tired at that time of day. Dinner has changed entirely in the South. Now you have dinner at night with everyone tired and half the family absent. But back in the Golden Age, when my children were growing up, we were still enjoying that fellowship and that rice and gravy and those vegetables stewed to a pleasant softness with that strip of bacon in there just as it should be. And at night, what did we eat? For the girls, the cook left a platter of sandwiches. As far as Ben and I were concerned, we didn't need any rich food after seven at night. We always had stale vanilla wafers and skim milk.

A Typical Southern Meal

WHEN I WAS A YOUNG HOSTESS IN THE EARLY 1950S, THE NOW FA-mous Historic Charleston Foundation was just getting started. They were trying to put together laws and directives that would control the changes being made to the old houses and even to keep those houses from being pulled down. In short, they wanted to prevent the destruction of old and beautiful things. But there wasn't a lot of know-how around. An organization in Philadelphia was doing similar work and was interested in seeing what Charlestonians had done, just as we were interested in getting advice from them. My husband, Ben Scott, was president of the Historic Charleston Foundation at the time.

Seventy-five people were coming from Philadelphia for the weekend. Invitations for lunch were parceled out and those without a specific reservation came to our house. Now our home tended to be a very casual establishment in those days. In the house were the three teenagers we were raising and also two warm and loving individuals who took care of all our important needs in the house and garden. But style and expertise had never been high up on our list of priorities. So as not to appear too down-to-earth that day, some last-minute teaching and polishing up were added to the warmth and willingness already there.

I got out the finger bowls, which I had inherited from a great-aunt, got them down from where they'd gathered dust for fifteen years, and seated at a perfectly laid-out single place setting, I went over and over the proper procedures for serving a Charleston midday dinner along with Ethel, our cook, and Lee, who often helped me in the yard and was going to help serve that day. The whole business seemed more or less opaque to me—unfathomable. It was as if the three of us were seated on Aladdin's carpet flying through the air on our way to cooking and serving lunch to the king of Siam. At the end of our practice session, we comforted each other and agreed that all would work out smoothly. We would proceed simply by taking a leap of faith and thinking positively. I'd just been reading Norman Vincent Peale's *The Power of Positive Thinking* at the time and felt that all we had to do was keep focused, think positively, and be everywhere at once.

I had decided that we would serve shrimp pie, red rice, green beans, and grapefruit and avocado salad—all of which Ethel could do with a hand tied behind her back. Nothing nerve-racking about any of that. For dessert we would serve the Lady Baltimore cake Charleston is famous for and I would make it. And we would start with mint juleps, which Ben would be responsible for. To be safe, we consulted three expert mint-julep makers and not surprisingly all three recipes turned out to be the same (you'll find it in Charleston's Junior League cookbook). I had a bed of mint in the garden, the start of which had been brought from the governor's mansion in New Bern, North Carolina. The most fragrant mint I've ever been near. Even today if my skirt brushes it as I walk by, I'm enveloped in this delicious strong fragrance. Mint is a part of the Charleston environment, part of the system.

The next hurdle was securing the original recipe for the Lady Baltimore cake. This was a closely guarded secret. The cake had been a staple at the Ladies Exchange, all of which was made famous by Owen Wister's novel *Lady Baltimore*. I got the recipe by promising never to pass it on, which I have not done until now. I got permission to publish it at long last and you'll find it on page 211.

I made that cake ahead of time, but on the morning of the dinner, with the number of guests suddenly rising, I realized I would need another. If I had been more experienced, I would have simply added ice cream to the menu and made the cake go round willy-nilly. But in those days I was more of a perfectionist. For me there were already too many ifs, ands, and buts about this affair to add shortage of cake to the list. So I cleared a corner in the kitchen, warned everybody not to talk to me, and set to it. I was making fast headway when my Uncle Nick and Name (my Aunt Em) appeared forty-five minutes early to check on the meal. When they saw me there with flour in my eyebrows, the kitchen about ninety-five degrees hot, and a drop of sweat on the end of my nose, they beat a hasty retreat to the garden and helped Ben greet the guests and serve the mint juleps.

A nerve-racking affair but we managed. I was using a blue-and-white Canton china and I borrowed more from Aunt Liz as the party grew. That Canton is what the blue willow pattern is a copy of, but the Canton is the stuff right from China. That table was lovely, all set with blue napkins, everything perfect. And the luncheon went off, in part, I suppose, because many in the room had been through the same sort of struggle themselves and had a fellow feeling for a young hostess.

And the mint juleps. The silver cups went in the freezer to give them a coating of ice and then they were served on a beautiful (and borrowed) old silver tray. (I don't like the word *antique*. *Old* is better.) We had borrowed more cups as well. And the mint juleps were a grand success and in a way less trouble than a bar would have been. We didn't have to go around saying, "Will you have wine? Will you have scotch? Will you have bourbon?" By damn, they were in the South. They had to drink a mint julep.

Edisto Seafood

BEN'S MOTHER WOULD LIVE WITH US FROM TIME TO TIME AND SHE WAS always welcome. I don't know the whole story of the Whaleys after the Civil War. Ben was the son of a Civil War veteran. His grandfather had enlisted at the beginning of the war and been wounded. The oldest son, Ben's uncle, should have been the next to go but he stayed home because he was interested only in "whiskey and women." So Ben's father, who was only sixteen, went to war. When he came back to the Carolina Low Country, it was to study law, but those were turbulent times in 1870s Charleston, during Reconstruction.

Naturally, Ben's father was a Southern Democrat and he had a disagreement with the Republican intendant—or, if you prefer, the carpetbagger mayor. So one morning in broad daylight on Broad Street, the mayor fired a shot at Ben's father and he returned fire. I've heard several accounts of what happened next, but the one that's written down is that the two men emptied their guns at each other, except that the mayor still had one bullet. He held his pistol barrel to Ben's father's forehead and said, "I'm giving you your life, now leave Charleston."

Ben's father went out to Alabama and practiced law there with some success. He practiced law down there until he was fifty-five and decided to come back to Edisto Island and plant cotton. Now, Ben's father had a brother, Uncle Eddings, who drank like a fish. He stayed tight as a monkey. Ben said he sang a little song, "Up in the stars, up in a balloon, very near the moon." He was the one who'd been interested only in whiskey and women. He wasn't about to take part in a war or much of anything else. He owned a plantation. He never had any children.

So fairly late in life, Ben's father came back and started planting one of his brother's islands. He was in a yawl—a small sailboat—coming back from this island when a storm came up, so he went into a creek—the entrance to Bohickett Creek, to be exact—tied up at a wharf, and went up to the house there and knocked on the door. And a beautiful young woman opened the door, the most beautiful young woman he'd ever seen, in fact. This was the future Mrs. Whaley, Ben's mother. She was twenty-one and he was fifty-five and they had four children, with Ben the youngest.

She was a wonderful cook. She was a master of something called bass-head stew. One of those big black iron pot recipes. As I've said, those pots were used for different purposes in different places in South Carolina, and on Edisto they made these wonderful fish stews. And Mrs. Whaley made this bass-head stew, which contained the heads of bass and the shoulders. Loads of onions. It was good, but I haven't had it in forty years.

While on the subject of Ben and his family and Edisto and food, I should definitely mention turtle eggs. You can't eat the eggs of loggerhead turtles today, which is as it should be. Those big seagoing turtles are endangered and have enough problems to contend with. But in the old days their eggs were considered a delicacy by many, especially when used in cakes—but eaten from the shell, too

Anyway, when Ben started being faced with gentlemen who wanted his beautiful daughters, this was one of his defenses. Ben loved turtle eggs because he'd grown up on Edisto Island. He had an old man bringing them from Edisto on a regular basis. They were nuggets of gold to Ben. I guess you don't know, but to eat them you pinch the eggs and then you sort of inhale them. The most disgusting procedure. The sound of sucking them was more than I could take. Ben didn't boil them. He ate them raw. I don't think it mattered, because even if you boil them they don't get hard. Awful. So our daughters' suitors, when faced with their prospective father-in-law for the first time, were offered raw turtle eggs. These young men had to eat them to be polite and they remember it with horror to this day. Oh, everybody knew Ben loved those eggs. Everywhere up and down the coast people brought them. Secret codes and oh, such carrying on, because even back then having the eggs was illegal—contraband. And Ben should have respected that, but he'd grown up surrounded by miles of empty beaches overrun with turtles and all manner of wildlife and just couldn't imagine a sea turtle becoming an object of scarcity.

Ivy Leaves for a Wedding Cake

BOUT 1980 OR SO, DIVORCES WERE FLYING AROUND TOWN LIKE BUZ-zards after some awful disaster. Though each week brought news of another separation, nothing had touched my own or my close friends' families. Then before you could say Jack Robinson, there we were, my good friend Louisa and my-self, witnessing three acrimonious failed relationships with six children involved.

Such a tragedy. We had absolutely no experience with any-thing like this. Nothing previous had taught us how to behave or deal with it. All situations seemed to have gone too far to correct and the tenet of the day seemed to be "Stand back, don't tam-per—this is the new order of things. What will be, will be."

Fine, but when the remarrying started, I looked for a rabbit's foot of sorts. I thought about the marriages that had taken place in Pinopolis and realized that indeed there was no divorcing going on among them. In fact, there had been no divorces of anyone in Pinopolis in my generation. So I started sifting over the events surrounding these occasions and I found my rabbit's foot: Cousin Deas Porcher had iced and decorated every one of our wedding cakes, and she'd decorated them with ivy leaves made of icing.

So on the first remarriage (Louisa's daughter, who was also my goddaughter), I suggested that Louisa make the cake herself (Louisa happens to be the best professional cake maker, in my opinion, in the entire Low Country) and that we decorate it with ivy leaves made of icing. "Yes, indeed, I said. "Let's set up every safeguard we can."

We did not have Cousin Deas's recipe for white icing. We tried out a few similar recipes. They were all dead failures. So then we got on the telephone and phoned every one of my friends who had had cakes made by Cousin Deas, thinking surely some of those girls would have the recipe. No luck. Not a soul knew. Louisa said, "We're going to manufacture those damn leaves. We'll just modify our own recipes." We tried several, again with very poor results.

Ben was so disgusted with us. He said, "Y'all have been over there again trying to make the icing go on. I never heard of anything so stupid." I said, "This is very important."

Oh, they were the worst-looking leaves. But the wedding was upon us and we determined to persevere with what we had, and we did. What we turned in was not a total failure, but it was also not a thing of beauty. Louisa looked at me and said, "Emily, if this were your daughter's cake, would you be satisfied?" And I said in my mind, Please, Lord, forgive me, but I'm about to give voice to a flat-out lie, and out loud, I said while icing the cake, "It certainly would suit me. It's very handsome. And I have a good feeling about it." I thought, That will settle that. And it did.

Well, "handsome" was a fairly accurate description. There was nothing delicate or gossamer about those ivy leaves, but let me say this, after more than ten years of wear and tear, that first remarrying still holds.

At the next ceremony (one of my girls), we produced the same clumsy result. But again the rabbit's foot has done its work and a year ago Louisa and I helped celebrate the tenth anniversary of that second remarriage. And in those ten years we've finally come up with a good recipe, so our cakes are now oohed and aahed over quite satisfactorily.

Both of us love to make and spend money and we might any day now go into the business of influencing successful marriages—any takers? Five dollars an ivy leaf. Well, I suppose we should let you do your own. What we have is a simple recipe (see page 227). It's not Cousin Deas's. In ours you use powdered sugar and egg whites. You don't cook it. You simply paint it on the back of leaves, real leaves—ivy, camellia, or whatever might be lucky for your bride and groom. Let the icing dry very thoroughly and then carefully peel away the real leaves.

Dancing School Fudge

I'M AN ENORMOUS GADGETEER. GADGETS FOR ME ARE WHAT LIQUOR IS FOR some people. I have to have the latest gadget for my kitchen. Ludicrous, I suppose, to want them all, but the search for convenience and tastiness continues to be a grand adventure.

Now, like everyone else I heard about this perfectly wonderful box called the microwave, but I had also heard all that stuff about how surely you would get cancer from the device and be dead before you reached the age of forty. Ben and I were at a judicial conference, and Sol Blatt was also there, one of the local federal judges, and his wife, Carolyn. They had been our friends for years and now Sol regaled us with his discovery. He said he couldn't live without his microwave. His hours were unpredictable, so Carolyn would simply leave a plate of dinner for him to warm up in this new kind of oven. It took only sixty seconds and didn't dry out the food.

When we all got home I called up Carolyn to see if what Sol had been telling every soul in three states was true. She invited me around to see for myself. That first afternoon we cooked chicken, asparagus, and custard. Everything came out perfect and delicious and at the end of the session she said, "Now, I'm going to give you the best recipe you ever had in your life and ever will get again." Which was microwave fudge. Into a china bowl she put a little can of evaporated milk, one stick of margarine, a cup of tiny marshmallows, sugar, and six ounces of chocolate bits. Then she stirred the whole thing up and put it in the microwave. After cooking, it hardened in ten minutes and was cut into perfect squares. Try it yourself if you don't believe me. The recipe's on page 203.

That microwave fudge became a great success at dancing school. We used it as a bribe. If a class wasn't going well, we'd announce the possibility of fudge next time: "Your doing the step by yourself is not going to get you a piece of fudge. You and your partner *both* have to be able to do that step. Either you both get a piece of fudge or neither does." Children and sweets do just go together, and the next week everybody would know the steps— magical. It became known as Dancing School Fudge and today many of our friends' children insist on Dancing School Fudge at their wedding receptions. I made it for my granddaughter Emily's wedding and that treat went as if sucked up into the air by a swift wind. Gone before I even got a piece.

Myrtle Allen

OWARD THE END OF HIS LIFE, BEN WAS NOT FEELING WELL AT ALL. HE needed to get away from everything that was around pressing in on him. We thought Ireland might be peaceful and so we asked our next-door neighbor Julia to recommend the best inn in Ireland, since she'd been to them all, and she said Myrtle Allen's. My daughters thought I was out of my mind—and it's true, that trip didn't turn out exactly right. But it served the purpose.

Ben was in a rolling chair and we took off from Charleston and flew to Ireland. Myrtle Allen's inn was located in a little village called Middleton, twenty-five miles to the north of Cork. I was seventy-two at the time and Ben was seventy-five and, as I said, not well. We landed in Shannon and then went to rent a car. They looked us over and said, "We don't rent to anybody who is over seventy." So Ben says, and he is just as quick as he could be, "Well, that's exactly what she is, seventy." Of course, at that point I looked eighty. They had diagnosed us immediately as a bad deal to rent a car to.

The drive was four hours and you have never seen anything

like those Irish roads (unless you too have been to Ireland). Twists and turns and potholes so big and deep that they swallow the car, and you're driving on the wrong side of the road. I never got over thirty-five miles per hour. Exhausting, but Ben did sleep most of the way.

We finally got there, to this ancient Irish house, and Ben was still doing okay. But I'd flown the whole day before and then driven four hours without even a bowl of soup. I went to sleep and they shook me awake at eleven the next morning for the most wonderful breakfast—mushrooms and tomatoes and eggs. They said they were concerned and had to see if we were still alive. We were.

Myrtle was running a four-star restaurant. She'd trained her chef, who wasn't but nineteen years old. Family-style meals were served with everybody invited in. Breakfast and dinner but no lunch except on Sundays. In the afternoon you were invited into the Allens' living room and Mr. Allen served drinks just as though he was having a party. The guests were from all over the place and at dinner you sat at tables of four or six or ten. And such dinners. Each one was a perfect delight and afterwards we sat on the adjoining terrace.

Myrtle had seven children, and what Ireland is noted for on the downside is unemployment. She kept them all busy, though. They grew all their own vegetables, quite an acreage. And she started a cooking school, which was run by a daughter-in-law. (Myrtle engineered space for me to attend this cooking school a couple of times when she was demonstrating: how you get the seeds out of a tomato and the proper way to mix bread dough, both of which I've forgotten.) She advertised that she could teach anybody to cook and to run an inn and she had thirteen or fourteen Irish girls being taught to run their own places.

Myrtle's orange marmalade was out of this world—out of Ireland, anyway. She sent to Spain for her oranges. The marmalade was itself almost a small industry. And in addition to this inn and its restaurant, she had a restaurant in Paris serving Irish food. She also had a cookbook out, *The Ballymaloe Cookbook*. I lent my copy out and can't remember to whom, so for the marmalade you'll have to get a copy on your own or go to Ireland and learn from Myrtle herself.

Ben and I kept the rented car and during the day we would drive all along the coast on those narrow, twisting dirt lanes. Delightful. We stayed for ten days doing these "day trips" and then what my daughters said would happen happened. Ben's fever spiked to 104 degrees. And the one thing Ben didn't want to do was to die away from home. I telephoned my daughter Miss Em and she managed, by hook or by crook, to get plane tickets for us immediately.

On that Irish plane they were wonderful about looking out for Ben and we got back to Charleston in one piece. If I had known that Ben would get that way I wouldn't have gone. But if we had stayed home, Ben and I would have missed ten grand days together. We would have missed the marmalade and the inn's little "retreat" cottage and its lagoon with white swans. So Irish. And we would never have met Myrtle Allen. Plain and simple, I love Ireland. I've been back twice to see the gardens and have discovered that Myrtle's isn't the only great place to eat. Every Irish inn I've been to has marvelous food.

Hoppin' John

OPPIN' JOHN—BACON AND COW-
PEAS AND RICE—IS SUPPOSED TO BE
a must at New Year's because without the peas you
might run into bad luck. But for once I thought I'd try to get
away from the same old New Year's Day menu. The family always had that first meal of the year at Fox Bank, our country
place up in Berkeley County. The menu was always turkey, roast
venison (see page 184), pilau, three vegetables, and, because
Anne liked it, a cranberry salad (see page 180), and then a green
salad with tomatoes and the rest. And, of course, hoppin' John
for luck.

That was the constant menu. Finally I decided it was just too
much and for Pete's sake, let's have fried chicken. I'm not standing over a turkey for four or five hours.

I suppose I should have gotten a second opinion. Or I should
have gone to Harris-Teeter and picked up a cooked turkey. But I
went on to Fox Bank and was ready at one o'clock. We had sandwiches, fried chicken, deviled eggs, and lemon pie. I thought it
was delicious. People could just take what they wanted from the
buffet and eat wherever they liked in the house.

But as it happened, every dog in the family was on the porch and a lot of people were out there, too, eating fried chicken. Grant Whipple left his plate for a second to refill his tea glass and what do you know, our dog Daisy grabs his chicken leg. And what do you know, my granddaughter Emily's beau tries to get the chicken leg out of Daisy's mouth and Daisy bites the fool out of him. And she hasn't had her rabies shot. When he gets back to Boston he becomes ill for three or four days and we get telephone messages coming in: What does the vet say about Daisy? Daisy has to be sequestered until we are sure she isn't rabid. Emily's beau recovers.

But the next year I went back to hoppin' John.

Charleston Seafood

HARLESTON IS SYNONYMOUS WITH SEAFOOD. WE HAVE ALL THESE WONderful restaurants and all of them are serving it. Every family has its special recipes. But I grew up forty miles inland on the banks of a freshwater swamp. We did not have seafood. All we had were freshwater bass and red breast bream. I had never seen a shrimp until I came to Charleston. I had never been faced with an oyster. When we were in Washington and Ben was working for Senator James Byrnes, my Aunt Cad telephones us and says, "I want you and Ben to come spend the weekend with us. I want you to meet some of my friends. I am sending you a train ticket. My chauffeur will meet you. Bring your good clothes — your party clothes."

So we get off the train in Philadelphia and sure enough — I had never seen such a car. Custom-made. A cream-colored Cadillac that would reach from here to King Street. Upholstered in buff blue, and who was at the wheel but a chauffeur with a cap and costume and somebody riding beside him in the same outfit. A footman? Whatever he was called, he was along to handle the baggage. The chauffeur wasn't expected to handle baggage, even though we were just coming overnight and had brought little.

Now Aunt Cad was a wonderful, rich personality. She looked like she had imbibed lots of clotted cream and all the best of everything else. She'd never held herself back. She must have weighed 185, wore her dresses to the ankles, and had the richest, most wonderful laugh. Like my father had. That laugh had the ring of a bell. Warm and outgoing. She just enveloped you with love and welcome.

Aunt Cad was waiting for us in her library in front of an open fire and beside her was a cocktail shaker of martinis. She said, "Ben, darling, I know that you must be exhausted after a day's work and we're ready to start festivities right now. I'm going to pour you a martini." A martini! I'd never heard of such a creation in my life. Had no idea what it was composed of. And of course, Cad could have drunk even Ben under the table. They each had two martinis. I had one, which had the most pleasant effect. We went upstairs to dress, then down to a dinner party of ten or twelve. The dinner was served in courses, which was a bit unsettling. And the first course, to my absolute horror, was oysters on the half shell. Oh my God, what will I do? I couldn't simply say I don't eat oysters. Don't ask me why I couldn't simply say that! So I manfully went through about three or four. Aunt Cad said, "Darling, I knew you and Ben would love these. They are a little bit bigger than our South Carolina oysters. They come from the Chesapeake Bay."

She was right about that. Tremendous, large oysters. But I mean, what is an oyster if you've been raised an entire forty miles from the ocean and never been exposed? I finally got through six. Hoped to God I would never see another raw oyster as long as I lived. I thought, I don't care what comes next. Everything is duck soup from here on out. Of course, there was silverware lined up on both sides of the plate and footmen and serving women everywhere and all this grand company. I was determined to behave appropriately. Then as I finished the last oyster, the man on my right, who I had never even glanced at because I was so occupied with the oysters, he said, "Ha, I don't eat oysters and I see how much you are enjoying them. You must have mine." Oh, my law. I had to eat half of his as well.

There's a moral here. Pass your oysters on to your neighbor before he can do the same to you or else relax and enjoy yourself and don't be afraid of offending your hostess. A good hostess simply wants you to enjoy yourself and won't care a whit if you refuse something as ungodly looking as an oyster.

Aunt Cad really was one of the outstanding hostesses in Philadelphia. She entertained beautifully and her conversational skills—well, if anybody came to the city who was difficult or important, Aunt Cad was invited out and seated next to that person. She had her box at the opera and went to the Friday-afternoon musicals and gave liberally to all musical enterprises. When Ben and I were there she took us to the opera. Ben had never been to one. When Aunt Cad came into her box the audience rose. That made an impression.

But I have truly wandered from the subject. I meant to be telling you about seafood and about Charleston, so I'll tell you about Ethel.

Ethel didn't have much respect for men. That's sad in a way, but not so very unusual. Ethel was our cook when the children were growing up and already old when she came looking for a job. She burst into tears when she got it. She was that thrilled to have work. She stayed with us for years. Her first husband had treated her badly and she didn't expect to take on another. She wasn't going to rely on any man.

Well, back in those ancient days, we still had street vendors calling their wares in the early morning and there was even a shrimp fleet that was nothing but small sailboats. I guess they used hand nets. Nothing like today's giant boats with their outriggers and winches. George was the name of the man who would come by our house with his shrimp singing his song every morning. "Shrimpies, shrimpies, raw, raw shrimp, shrimp." Shrimp! Unending shrimp. Cost twenty-five cents a plate. A tin plate piled up. The heads still on them. Charlestonians always had shrimp for breakfast. In those days the shrimp man came about seven o'clock. We'd just be waking. At quarter to seven St. Michael's bells rang and we'd hear the shrimp man coming down the street singing.

I noticed we were having a lot of shrimp in the house and that

Ethel had started singing herself. All day long she was singing around the kitchen. Then one day while serving she says with a grin, "I'm getting married." "Who to?" we ask. Who else could it be? George the shrimp man. We were so thrilled for her. And at the wedding we met George's Yale-graduate grandson, who was dressed in a gray flannel suit. And Ethel herself had a very gifted daughter who became the breakfast cook for the King Charles Hotel. You have to be good to be the breakfast cook. Which does show how things change from generation to generation, and for the good in many ways.

Restaurants

⸻◈⸻

I LOVE FRIED FLOUNDER. CREIGHTON FRAMP-
TON, WHO IS NINETY-TWO YEARS OLD, TAKES
me out to lunch if I jog his memory. And we always go to
California Dreaming and I always, without hesitation, order
fried flounder. California Dreaming serves the most delicious
fried flounder you ever put in your mouth. Perfect each and
every time. Fresh and delicious. I know it's a chain restaurant and
that we have all these other wonderful restaurants in Charleston
and that Charlestonians usually don't take to chains. Plus this one
is located all the way across the Ashley River. But California
Dreaming is worth the trip.

The place is always full of young people, a tremendous variety
of people. And very noisy. I pull my chair up to Creighton. I get
my right ear up to him, my good ear. I order a glass of wine. We
always have a grand time. We always order the fried flounder.
And fried potatoes. When we go in there we're not going to eat
a damn thing but fried food and a couple glasses of wine.

You know, it's not fair not to give places a chance. That old
Greek restaurant on King Street is closed now, but as I've said,
Ben and I used to drive by just to see the chickens turning on the

grill in the window. Just turning and turning. And we never went in.

Oh, we have wonderful food in Charleston. But I suspect I'd be in trouble for mentioning one or two places and leaving the others out. Let's just say it's hard to go wrong. Our restaurants can be crowded, though. Charleston is filling up with people and we have a city full of students, but that's also the reason we now have the great restaurants. When the tea olives break into bloom and the smell is so delicious everywhere and the loquat is blooming at the same time and the crab cakes are sautéing, isn't this city an absolutely wonderful place to be?

What Rosie Eats

ACH BREED OF DOG COMES WITH ITS SPECIAL TALENTS, WHAT YOU MIGHT CALL the "nature" of that breed. When Nan could no longer ride or even walk in the woods, she would sit in a chair outside and listen to her beagles running rabbits behind the house. She simply took pleasure in their voices and in the pleasure they received from running rabbits, which is the nature of the beagle, for they are the rabbiting breed.

In the old, old days we kept all sorts of dogs. In the yard would be eight to fifteen hounds. We had foxhounds and always two or three deer dogs plus two or three bird dogs. Those last were the pointers and Dad trained them with the utmost care. He never left the table that he didn't take a little piece of the relish, ham or whatever it was. He'd go outside and call his bird dogs to him. Dad would get down on his haunches eye to eye with those dogs three times a day. He taught those dogs how to heed, how to hi on. He'd hold that relish right under a dog's nose and say "heed, heed, heed" and if that dog didn't heed his ear would be pinched. And when Dad got to "hi on," then the dog could have the little piece of meat.

When you are bird hunting you cannot have a dog who doesn't answer to "heed." An undisciplined dog will go ahead of you and flush a covey of quail before you are within gunshot. As the dog heeds, the man has to walk up and flush the birds. The dog is not to break shot. The dog has to stand behind the hunter or the operation collapses. Now, a dog at point is a beautiful sight. It's his nature to freeze when the birds are near, lift his tail, and point his nose in the direction of the covey. I'm telling you this so that you will understand that each breed of dog has its talents, talents for which it has been bred over hundreds of years.

My dog, Rosie, is a Jack Russell terrier and Jack Russells are the willful breed. And Rosie is an outstanding Jack Russell. She won't come to call. She manages to boss me completely. Last night my grandson Ben and I sang and played at the piano and Rosie came and demanded, in the most imperious way, that we stop the racket. The postman is her mortal enemy. She waits for him every day. Fortunately he is used to her by now and I still get my mail delivered. She is willful and totally self-directed and worst of all she will not eat cooking failures. Rosie is very particular about what she eats. If I fail at a recipe, I can't simply scrape it into her dish. She will not eat what has been improperly cooked. And she will not eat dog food for hell. So when I cook now I cook for both of us. Cream of wheat, poached eggs, whatever, I just cook two of everything. But in my defense, I will say that I never cook anything especially for her. Rosie must eat what I eat.

Poaching an Egg for a Man

AS I MENTIONED, MY MOTHER, NAN, TOLD ME MANY YEARS AGO THAT THE way to a man's heart is through his stomach, and I believed her then and still do think it is certainly one of the straighter avenues.

Ben Scott loved poached eggs. To make the egg come out in one piece, just put a spoonful of vinegar in the simmering water, and swirl the water in the pan, and drop the egg in the middle. Once cooked, you remove the egg with a spoon that has holes, place it on a paper towel, then on a piece of buttered toast. Which is the old way. I have a new gadget now that has two "bowls" and you put a teaspoon of water in each one, put your eggs in, clamp the top down, and put them in the microwave. They slide out of their bowls straight onto the toast. A couple of my grandsons love poached eggs and I fix them whenever they're around.

I have to admit, though, that for the last two years they haven't asked me to do this. They're getting up past thirty. All their young lives I'd cook poached eggs, put the eggs on toast, and set the plates on the table in front of them. And then they'd say, "Now Cheeka, please cut into this egg for me. It tastes good the way you cut it." I guess at their current advanced ages they're ashamed to ask me to cut up their breakfast, or maybe a fear of feminist retaliation has taken hold, or maybe they've gotten too knowledgeable about how they'll die from eating too many poached eggs. At any rate, they've stopped asking, which is a shame, since I enjoyed the entire ceremony.

White Mountain Icing
and the Vitiated Taste Buds

WHEN I WAS A CHILD LIVING IN PINOPOLIS, MY MOTHER'S AUNT Miss Caroline Sinkler would send us a beautiful and delicious cake at Easter. I always wondered how those cakes arrived in such pristine condition, coming as they did all the way from Philadelphia. That wonder of my childhood was called a White Mountain Cake and from those days until this afternoon I had never come across that confection anywhere else. Succulent and flavored with almond. This A.M. I was glancing through some untried recipes and staring me in the face was White Mountain Icing (see the recipe on page 225). I went straight into the kitchen and despite the weather, which didn't look promising for icing, gathered up the ingredients and set forth on the avenue to my childhood. And the cake worked and was as lovely to look at as when I was nine years old, except . . . except for the difference.

During the First World War, sugar had been rationed and anything sweet was a treasure and spoken of at length. Now we have all the sugar we want and in every imaginable form. And now at eighty-seven my taste is more sophisticated and my taste buds probably just a bit jaded. As a child, I remember Nan saying to me as I sprinkled a bit more salt on my food, "No! Don't do that! You'll vitiate your taste buds!" And me wondering, What the hell do you mean by that? She was right, I suppose. My taste buds probably are vitiated. White Mountain Icing, though of a perfect shiny-cloud consistency, was too bland in the original recipe. So I have added a twist here—a taste of lemon—which brings it back to my childhood dreams. You may join me there.

And in case you're wondering, as I did, according to *Webster's* dictionary, *vitiate* means "to make faulty or defective, often by the addition of something that impairs." Oh yes, and the second definition: "to debase in moral or aesthetic status." I suppose both definitions suit.

House Parties

OOKING BACK ON MY LIFE, IT SEEMS TO ME THAT HOUSE PARTIES ARE LIKE church steeples in a cityscape. Gathering congenial people together for two or three nights, men and women usually, was the most fun. Ben and I would sometimes even double up with another couple and use two houses.

Football weekends, those were money in the house-party bank, and the same is so of basketball games these days, especially for family gatherings. Anyone who doesn't want to watch "the game" plays bridge or takes walks, whatever—picnics, swimming—just fun together.

Now here's my notion of a perfect Charleston-based house party. What's required? An at-ease hostess (and host) waiting on the front porch. No breathless last-minute stuff allowed. Everything must be comfortably in place. You're giving yourself a party as well. And what good is all the preparation if you can't be at ease welcoming your guests?

There should be a touch of luxury. Bowls of fresh flowers in the living room. Two or three rosebuds make a hit in the bedrooms. New magazines to idle with. There should be new, inspiring, and much talked of books within reach. Soft drinks, plenty of ice, and snacks in convenient locations. Every bedroom should have a vacuum pitcher of ice water and glasses and napkins, and the beds should be obviously luxurious looking. Small soft pillows, colorful throws to snuggle under for a short nap. In the bathroom a cake or so of Yardley's English Lavender and a fresh box of Kleenex.

When you've produced a touch of luxury, a touch of style, and possibly a sense of happy anticipation, your guests will begin to feel that maybe they are going to be spoiled a bit. When they are leisurely unpacking, showering, and changing from their traveling clothes, you have time to get the cocktails and hors d'oeuvres out. All of this is adding up to *unhurried*.

The table has been set, the food is the kind that needs only a little bit of last-minute attention to be ready exactly when we seem to be ready. The guests can follow you into the kitchen and help pour the water, uncork the wine, everyone has a little job to help make him part of the logistics. A perfect number for these house parties is six guests, eight including the host and hostess. Eight is good because you have built-in golf, tennis, or bridge teams or a nice number for poker.

Supper is served buffet-style and the dessert sits beside the hostess within easy reach. The coffee and chocolates will have been put on an out-of-the-way table in the living room before the guests arrive. (Thermos coffeepots are wonderful assets.) Although I do warn against letting guests help, *house-party* guests may help put dishes in the dishwasher, then all will adjourn to the living room for coffee, conversation, and chocolates, plus liqueurs if desired.

At 8:00 A.M. you should have breakfast. Though you can manage a weekend like this without a cook, in the morning it is wonderful to have some help for two or three hours—to empty the dishwasher, refill the ice buckets, collect used glasses, straighten the bar, throw out half-used tonic-water and soft-drink cans, empty the trash cans, bring in the newspapers, etc.

On Saturday midday, you should have a picnic lunch on the porch, nap, and then walk around town to see gardens and houses of architectural interest or drive over the Charleston bridges to view the town and rivers from high up.

Saturday night, perhaps bring in another couple, unless you already have the perfect number for bridge or poker. Have your experienced help return to set the table and put out your already prepared hors d'oeuvres and cheeses and set up the buffet table. Always serve buffet-style. And after the meal, a repeat of the coffee, conversation, and chocolates, and then some games.

On Sunday morning I like to offer bowls of icy cold cut-up fruit served with bacon and eggs. Coffee cake. Have the help turn up once again if possible. Then walk or attend whatever church has a good choir and minister, take everybody to lunch at a good restaurant, and then adieu.

The tumult and the shouting dies, the Captains and the Kings have departed. A house party of this caliber could be wrapped up as an especially delightful Christmas present to your closest friends.

A Serious Admonition That I'm Totally Positive About

⸺◦◉◦⸺

DON'T SERVE GUESTS DISHES YOU HAVEN'T MADE SUCCESSFULLY TWO OR THREE TIMES —and quite lately. When the special evening comes, you need to be comfortable with the food you are serving and with the way it is being served. If you're treating yourself to help, practice with them until you're sure they know what is expected and they are comfortable and at ease doing it. After all, I generally give a party for my own pleasure as well as my guests' pleasure and I'm not about to ruin my occasion by being jittery. What experience has taught me is that people consider it a special compliment to be invited to a meal. If the hostess is all aflutter like a butterfly caught in a net, then, as the Irish say, "I wish I was to home and the party was to hell!"

If possible, ask people for "supper" rather than for "dinner." Supper is more casual, more relaxed, and these days dinner implies something pretty top drawer—a meal that would require a maid and a butler, best evening clothes, all of which threatens stiffness instead of stylishness.

If you are cooking *and* serving, choose the entrée and the dessert from a list of things that can be cooked the day before.

Ones I particularly turn to are Marty's Pork Tenderloin (page 172) and Priscilla's Chicken (page 162). I think of recipes like these as "hostess friendly," dishes that cook in a certain length of time and don't need a mother hen to watch over them.

If you do not have someone to serve, have a buffet in the dining room. Guests usually feel comfortable getting up for a second helping. When supper is over, leave the dishes on the table, blow out the candles, shut the door, and serve finger desserts and coffee in another room, with hostess and host doing the serving. (These days I've found that grandsons also do quite well.) Do not let your supper guests help you clean up. Give them a treat from start to finish. And do not do so much work the day of the party that you are really tired by evening. For instance, don't do the flowers on the day of the party. Use a few rosebuds brought in two days earlier and arranged with greens. By the night of the party they will be half open and very lovely. Or treat yourself to those beautiful big white lilies that last a week or ten days. Make brownies a week ahead and freeze them or buy delicious chocolates and serve Irish coffee. Just a small amount of personal experience will have you doing it all without a hitch.

Here are suggestions for easy and tasty combinations that I feel are successful. Serve one meat or seafood, one starch, one vegetable, one salad, and one dessert with coffee, and make sure there is plenty of everything. You cut down on the number of pots, the number of serving dishes, supper dishes, and dessert dishes. And when your guests have departed, you can get every-thing into your one dishwasher. A big plus.

Why do I like to invite people for a meal—for a supper, a party, a weekend house party? Because I know no better way to speed and enrich friendships. It's true, friendships can't be hurried, but they can be tended, and tending them has a great payback, for you've no time left for stewing in your own self-centered juices. Oh, life is pretty forlorn without friends, both old and new. Collect them. Congenial people, ones who are trustworthy and accountable and productive—and especially those who have a sense of humor.

It's a challenge to focus all your skills on bringing together the right assemblage of guests, food, table settings, and flowers. Nothing elaborate, but colorful and convenient, with you as the relaxed/warm/welcoming hostess or host. Can you pull this off without the fuss and feathers showing? Without the hurry, scurry, and flurry? A gamble! It certainly is, but I love to gamble, and even the best-laid supper plans come with a question mark attached. The result is always a mystery, in the lap of the gods.

Emily's Wedding

S I SAID, WE MADE DANCING SCHOOL
FUDGE FOR THE BRUNCH I GAVE AT
my granddaughter Emily's wedding. And we'd
planned for shrimp and hominy. The caterer couldn't handle
that, so I went down to Edisto and bought fifty pounds of shrimp
off the dock. And Margaret peeled all fifty pounds without stopping. Then, managing two pans at once, we started up my
mother-in-law's sauce, the recipe given on page 108—not really
a tomato sauce—green pepper and onion and butter instead of
bacon drippings.

That shrimp and hominy brought down the house, all two
hundred souls. That fifty pounds disappeared. Such a warm and
happy celebration, that wedding feast. It is very basic, the breaking of bread, the being together, it cements friendships whether
it's a simple meal or a wedding party. A hastening of friendships,
a reaching out—the feast at Cana. And at the reception that or-
chestra was cutting loose. "Mack the Knife" full blast. Everybody
really moving. If they hadn't played wide open, Miss Em would
have seen that they did.

Two of the LeClercq boys and their father, Fred, were all out on the floor. They each carved out about ten square feet. Coattails flying. Neckties flying. The girls flying. You never saw such dancing.

But the youngest, Kershaw, still hasn't learned to dance and his date wasn't pleased with that. I've been trying to teach Kershaw to dance since he was five years old. I am a professional dance instructor and yet I have failed miserably with him and don't know why. After the wedding I took him to the airport and came home and went to bed. The next morning I came down and found this thing draped over the sofa, much more dead than alive. None of him that wasn't wrinkled. Decayed around the edges. You never saw such a disheveled mortal in your life. He'd missed the plane, then come home for a couple hours of sleep, and the door had closed on him, locking him out, so he'd slept the night in my car. Someone let him in early in the morning. I drove him back to the airport a second time and as a reward he promised to let me teach him how to dance.

Oh, all my grandchildren are great fun.

The Holy Grail

I'M CLEANING OUT MY CHARLESTON KITCHEN. THE CARPENTERS ARE COMING. This room hasn't seen a carpenter in fifty years. Cleaning out this room we've found everything but twins in a coffin. We've found my mother's utensils. We've found *her* mother's utensils. We've found Uncle Nick's mother's utensils. But of course the bulk of the debris is my own.

I can't help it. I'm a collector of gadgets. A gadgeteer. Look at what I have out on the counter and up on the shelves and in the drawers.

Let's start with the electric mixer. Mine is a KitchenAid but the mixer part doesn't move up and down; I'd really prefer one that is hinged. I have a Cuisinart on the counter as well, but it doesn't whip eggs. I use my blender as much as the Cuisinart. You add an attachment and you can make a cheese dip—two kinds of cheese softened with sherry. In any case, you need all three gadgets.

This flour sifter is new. I try out everything. Whatever will add to the quickness of cooking. A plastic cap on the bottom of the sifter so the flour doesn't fall through when you're measuring. A very helpful gadget.

A brand-new lemon zester. With a regular zester—a sort of grater—your knuckles are in there, too. Human flesh and lemon rind.

An electric can opener. Mine's a Sunbeam. A crank one will serve if you're pressed for room.

A big handle. The difference between a good and a bad apple corer. Bigger handle. Remember that.

And the best gadget in a kitchen is a sharp knife. My sister had a very trusty husband. His job in the kitchen was to keep every knife as sharp as it could be.

An electric orange squeezer (if you have the room).

An electric knife. I always keep the serrated blade in mine.

A cutting board—built-in or otherwise—and a surface to put hot pots on.

And amongst my most prized possessions is this plastic silverware holder. A tall cylinder with graduated compartments for each type of service.

An asparagus server.

A gadget to pour tea through—a new-type strainer.

A MICROWAVE. The biggest boon to cooks in history. This one is a Sharp. It's a convection oven, broiler, and microwave in one. It can cook high and low, slow and fast. In the convection mode, a loaf of bread cooks in three-quarters of the time as in a regular oven and it cooks perfectly.

Rubbermaid canisters. Leftover cereal in every one.

A relic from the Stone Age—a small toaster oven that we still use for toasting sandwiches.

Here's one that's brand-new. A bacon triangle. You hang your bacon on this triangle and then slip it into the microwave.

An open-the-jar gadget. A broad funnel. A wonderful hand-operated eggbeater. Pyrex and more Pyrex. A sturdy pair of scissors to cut up chicken or strip ham easily.

Nothing invented compares to a paper towel.

Oh, there are all sorts of time-savers out there. Just in the way food is pre-prepared nowadays—half mixed or more when you take it from the store. Jiffy muffin mix is a must. New flavors every day and the name Jiffy tells you it's fast. At the supermarket you buy your bag of lettuce already washed and cut and ready to go into the salad. All this saves so much time. Pam in a spray can.

Plus, there's the layout of the kitchen. They have time studies, efficiency studies, done now by engineers. How many steps to the stove? How many to the refrigerator? That's never been a problem in my kitchens, since they were all small to start with. Not that I wouldn't want a large kitchen—even one with easy chairs and a TV. It's just that I don't want anybody at the stove with me. I don't want anybody butting into me. Even at our country place, Fox Bank, I laid out the kitchen so that it's best if only one cook is behind the counter at a time. I like it that way. Selfish. Everything should be in its place and if anybody else is messing around back there that won't happen. Open shelves help. That's a simple aid. And keeping what you need most often waist high and the lesser-used either up or down—but all of this is just common sense.

The only problem with speeding up work in the kitchen is with the gadget inventors themselves. They've come up with the most extraordinary things. A West Bend slow cooker. You can put a ham in and leave it for a couple of hours, or cook rice or banana bread in it. The microwave can do absolutely anything and you don't have to watch it or tote three kinds of firewood to it. Yes, inventors obviously know how to invent. The problem is, they all seem to be recluses. They don't understand entertaining.

I'm going to contact one of these people myself. The Daisy company has a good-looking frying pan with a white dome. You can control the heat, cook an entire meal in it, put it warm on the table, go out on the porch and have a couple of cocktails, and then announce to your guests that they may enter and serve themselves and be confident that the meal will be delicious and attractive. Still, this handsome product has some serious flaws that I'd be happy to help them out with. We could make it perfect.

My daughters tease me and say it's the Holy Grail I'm searching for. Maybe. But it does seem ridiculous to me. They can put a man on the moon and keep a dog from barking with an electric collar. That can mean only one thing. Kitchen-gadget inventors don't know how to entertain or don't care to. They sit at home eating soup from a can. They're not gregarious or outgoing at all. I need to meet one. I can make him understand.

Pilaus

ILAUS ARE ONE-POT MEALS. AROUND HERE WE PRONOUNCE IT "PUR-LOW." Okra. Red rice. Ham. Chicken. Oh, anything at all can go in the pilau pot—an old, old Southern tradition left over from log-cabin days. Well, when Ben Scott and I were planning our getaway house at Fox Bank, we hired a crew of local Berkeley County men to build it. And one of the two top carpenters always had a little gas stove going on the front porch and from that pot came the most divine smells. He used turkey necks and rice and then all sorts of other things went into that pot. That crew, black and white, old and young, worked together in such harmony. I always suspected it was because they were eating from that same pot.

They started building the house in the bitter cold, January 2, and were finished March 2, and I believe that pilaus were the key to their swift success. What's put me in mind of all that, I suppose, is the work being done on my kitchen in town now and what I said at the beginning of this book about the air in kitchens. I said that the air in kitchens can be mysteriously nurturing. I said that if you believed a cubicle of space could emanate an ambience, then I was certain the air in kitchens was entirely different from the air anywhere else in the house. Well, I'm not taking that back now — just part of the way back.

My own kitchen is now completely upside down. My daughter Marty and I have had it pulled apart, and what's not apart is being freshly painted. This too will pass, I remind myself. But not immediately.

The new appliances didn't fit in the assigned places. And the linoleum had been torn up and half replaced before we realized that the new color didn't look the same as the patch in the showroom looked. All of this had gone on weeks too long and now, as I'm telling you this, we're well into April. Yesterday, just as one of the most important garden tours was beginning in my garden behind the house, a giant truck arrived at the front and blocked narrow little Church Street while they delivered four new cabinets. Meanwhile, the touring guests were already being greeted with the sight of my old ripped-out stove and washing machine propped up outside the service door. So the temporarily not so serene and nurturing air of the kitchen is now intruding upon the serene and nurturing air of the garden. What a mess.

This too will pass. When the king asked the wise men to come up with the absolutely most profound piece of wisdom to be inscribed inside his ring, that's what they gave him. I've said it so often that now my grandson Ben is also claiming, "This too will pass."

It came as a surprise when I was recently asked to speak on

the subject of old age. You see, this was the first time I had to really accept—or even thought—that I was in that category. But I must be. I've got to admit that eighty-seven doesn't figure out as middle age. All right, I'm no longer middle-aged anymore. But this categorizing of where old age starts and what it looks like should be kicked overboard. It seems to me that as long as we are physically independent and open to absorbing new and different ways of doing things and incorporating these new ways into our everyday life, then we qualify as viable, productive humans. Old age! It's simple. We don't feel old if we're physically not in pain.

I had a visitor in the garden last week, a delightful gentleman who, when searching in vain for the right word, said of his lapse of memory, "I'm having a senior moment." Now there is a piece of wisdom I'm certainly glad to have, for I have many such moments myself. My parents taught me this: You will be given as much as you give. My visitor with his "senior moment" gave me a new and very handy phrase at the same time that he was reassuring both himself and me that we are not alone in this world. And I do hope what I have to say here about cooking and entertaining and raising children and being raised ourselves will strike a sympathetic chord in the same way.

I have been lucky. I was given a head start by my parents. And by the small community of Pinopolis, where I spent the first twenty-three years of my life. My parents were certain of their values. What they valued was honesty, kindness, and productivity. They were Roosevelt Democrats. They were democrats, plain and simple, and accepted all human beings. And they were undeviating in their commitment to their family and their community. When something had to be attended to, they didn't wait for others to do the attending. They gathered up help and acted. It was my good fortune to come from such parents, and the good fortune of my own children to know them as well.

And to repeat, here is what I was taught. WE should help and encourage others to reach their full potential, for if they are brought to their full potential and we are brought to our full potential, then civilization will inch forward a notch or two. I myself am responsible for seeing that anyone who touches my life will get my support. This decision is not altogether altruistic. I want people to succeed for the good of us all. I want their self-confidence not to be beaten down and denied. Trust and enthusiasm and support are the best things all of us have to offer, our products, you might say. They do not always take the form of words. We can cook these products in the kitchen, we can grow them in our gardens. But whatever the form, when we give our best products we are giving love. Love is made up of many parts (like a good cake recipe, I'm tempted to say)—comfort, compassion, loyalty, encouragement, companionship, pleasure.

Love is a fine sauce! Have you heard that? I suppose it means that anything tastes great if you're in love. Well, that may be true, but romance is not exactly the kind of love I am talking about here, or rather it's only a part of that love. What's coming next are about a hundred of my favorite recipes. Some of them are easy. I hope you'll try my hard ones, as well. Perseverance is a fine sauce, too.

Watch the oven settings. Play it by ear.

And 100 Recipes from
a Charleston Kitchen

Breakfast and Brunch Dishes

Grits

We call it grits when it's in the box at the grocery store and these same grits are called hominy when we have cooked it for an hour. Regardless of the instructions on the box, we in the South hope our hominy has been cooked for an hour. It's creamy and delicious and goes with everything from eggs and bacon to shrimp, sausage, venison meatballs, fried whiting—you name it, we like it with hominy.

The easiest way to cook grits is in a rice steamer. If you don't have one, you can improvise (see page 174).

1 cup grits
1 teaspoon salt
4 ½ cups water

Put plenty of water in the bottom of a rice steamer; you don't want it to boil away. In the top of the steamer, stir together the grits, salt, and 4 ½ cups water. Put the cover on and let the water in the bottom of the steamer come to a boil. When it has been boiling for a few minutes, uncover the top of the steamer, stir the grits, and re-cover. In another 10 to 15 minutes, stir again, recover, and turn the heat to low. The hominy should be ready to eat in about 30 to 45 minutes.

VARIATION: Grits can also be cooked in a heavy nonstick pot with a tight lid. For this method, bring 4 cups water and 1 teaspoon salt to a rolling boil. Pour in 1 cup grits in a steady stream, stirring constantly until the hominy has thickened. If you don't stir constantly, the hominy will be lumpy. When it has thickened, cover the pot, turn the heat to low, and let the hominy simmer for about 20 minutes, until all the water is absorbed. While it simmers, it won't require much attention, but I think it's smart to keep your eye on it and to stir occasionally.

Serves 4 people.

Edisto Breakfast Shrimp

Edisto Island is one of the sea islands, a still surprisingly remote and unspoiled spot about forty miles south of here. I guess if it's famous for anything besides some wonderful cooks and cooking, it's for the size of its extended families, of which the Whaleys were one. This recipe is from Ben's mother. I always think of her as Mrs. Whaley.

I used to use bacon drippings instead of butter for this recipe, and it's tastier that way. It's also very good with cream, especially when spooned over hominy.

3 tablespoons unsalted butter
1 medium onion, chopped (about ½ cup)
¼ green pepper, chopped
2 tablespoons all-purpose flour
1 pound uncooked shrimp, peeled
1 teaspoon salt
Generous dash of Tabasco
1 teaspoon Worcestershire sauce
4 tablespoons tomato ketchup (more to taste)
2 tablespoons chopped fresh parsley
½ cup heavy cream (optional)

1. Melt the butter in a medium sauté pan over medium heat. Add the onion and green pepper and cook until tender but not brown. Stir the flour into the mixture and let bubble a minute.

2. Turn up the heat and add the shrimp, stirring until they are pink, about 2 minutes. Add enough water to almost cover the shrimp and stir until the mixture has thickened a bit. Add the salt, Tabasco, Worcestershire sauce, ketchup, and parsley and stir. Let the mixture simmer for about 5 minutes. Adjust the seasonings to taste.

3. Stir in the heavy cream if desired. Do not let the mixture come to a boil once the cream has been added, but heat thoroughly. Serve immediately.

Serves 4 people.

Breakfast Dish for a House Party

Leftover French bread works really well in this recipe. I assemble it the night before and then bake it in the morning. It can also be frozen after being assembled and then defrosted when the time comes to bake it. Serve with fruit and coffee for a delicious breakfast.

1½ pounds small pork sausages
2 tablespoons unsalted butter
2 cups sliced mushrooms
6 slices white bread, torn into pieces
8 ounces grated sharp Cheddar cheese
2½ cups milk

4 large eggs, well beaten
1 10 ½-ounce can cream of mushroom soup
1 small onion, grated
¼ teaspoon ground black pepper
⅛ teaspoon dried thyme

1. Place the sausages in a skillet with ½ cup water, cover, and cook over medium heat for 3 minutes. Uncover and continue cooking for 15 minutes or until the sausages are golden brown. Drain on paper towels and set aside.

2. In a large skillet, melt the butter and sauté the mushrooms until they are wilted and any liquid has evaporated. Remove from the heat and set aside.

3. In a large bowl, combine the bread, cheese, milk, eggs, soup, onion, pepper, and thyme. Set aside.

4. Combine the sausages and mushrooms and transfer to a 9" × 13" casserole dish. Pour the cheese mixture over the sausages and mushrooms, cover with plastic wrap, and refrigerate overnight.

5. In the morning, preheat the oven to 350°F. Take the casserole out of the refrigerator, remove the plastic wrap, and bake in the preheated oven for 1 hour. Serve immediately.

Serves 8 people.

Virginia Spoon Bread

More trouble than hominy bread, this is an old, old recipe from the Virginia side of my family, from back when "hostess friendly" would have been confused with "friendly hostess." This dish is tricky because you have to serve it like a soufflé—that is, immediately.

3 cups water
3 cups yellow cornmeal
6 tablespoons unsalted butter or margarine
4 cups milk
3 large eggs
1 tablespoon salt
3 heaping teaspoons baking powder
1 tablespoon sugar

1. Preheat the oven to 375°F and grease a 7" × 10" casserole dish. Set aside.

2. Bring the water to a boil and slowly stir in the cornmeal. Reduce the heat to medium and keep stirring until the mixture is smooth. Add the butter or margarine and stir until it melts. Gradually add the milk, stirring constantly so that the cornmeal does not become lumpy. Stir in the eggs, salt, baking powder, and sugar.

3. Turn the cornmeal into the prepared casserole dish and bake in the preheated oven for 1 hour. Serve immediately.

Serves 8 to 10 people.

Rice and Hominy Muffins

This recipe was once an important part of every Southern cook's repertoire. They served rice or hominy every one of the 365 days of the year, so there was usually some leftover rice or hominy to be used for these muffins, which were a nice change from cornbread, Sally Lunn, and yeast rolls. The amount of rice or hominy doesn't have to be exact—anywhere from a cup to a cup and a half works fine.

1 cup all-purpose flour
4 teaspoons baking powder
¼ teaspoon salt
1 tablespoon sugar
4 tablespoons unsalted butter, melted
2 large eggs, well beaten
1 cup milk
1–1½ cups cooked rice or hominy, or a combination of both

1. Preheat the oven to 425°F and grease enough muffin tins to make 12 regular-size muffins. Set aside.

2. In a large bowl, sift together the flour, baking powder, salt, and sugar. Set aside.

3. In a medium bowl, combine the melted butter, eggs, and milk, then stir into the flour mixture. Stir in the rice and/or hominy. Pour the batter into the prepared muffin tins and bake in the preheated oven for 25 minutes. Allow to cool just a little before serving.

Makes 12 muffins.

Catherine's Waffles

You're indulging yourself when you eat these, though Dad ate them every morning for breakfast. In those days, Catherine cooked them in a cast-iron waffle iron on top of the old wood-burning stove. Imagine how expert she had to be to stoke the fire to just the right temperature. And the wood box had to have the right amount and type of wood to allow her to accomplish this seven days a week!

1¾ cups all-purpose flour
4 teaspoons baking powder
1 teaspoon salt
1 tablespoon sugar
2 large eggs, well beaten
1½ cups milk
8 tablespoons unsalted butter, melted

1. In a large bowl, sift together the flour, baking powder, salt, and sugar.

2. In a medium bowl, thoroughly combine the eggs, milk, and melted butter. Add gradually to the dry ingredients, beating well after each addition. You don't want lumpy batter. Make sure your waffle iron is well greased and hot before you spoon the batter into it.

Makes 4 waffles.

Little Thin Cornmeal Pancakes

These were always served for breakfast at High Hills in Flat Rock when Nan was mistress there. They are delicious with honey.

1½ cups water
1 cup yellow cornmeal
2 tablespoons bacon drippings or unsalted butter
1 tablespoon sugar
1 large egg, well beaten
½ cup all-purpose flour
1 teaspoon salt
¾ teaspoon baking powder
¾ cup milk

1. Bring the water to a boil in a large saucepan. Slowly add the cornmeal, stirring constantly. Continue to stir until thickened, about 5 minutes. Remove from the heat.

2. Add the bacon drippings or butter, the sugar, and the egg. Combine thoroughly.

3. In a medium bowl, sift together the flour, salt, and baking powder. Stir this mixture into the cornmeal in two parts, alternating with enough milk to make a batter the consistency of corn syrup (you may need more than ¾ cup milk).

4. Ladle ¼ cup of the batter onto a hot, buttered griddle for each pancake. They will be very thin. Cook for about 2 minutes, until bubbles form on the top. Flip and cook the other side for another 2 minutes or so. Serve immediately.

Makes about 12 small pancakes.

Banana-Nut Bread

The bananas should be ripe, but not rotten. You don't have to watch over this one very closely.

6 tablespoons unsalted butter, at room temperature

¼ cup sugar

1¼ cups mashed ripe banana (about 3 bananas)

1 teaspoon fresh lemon juice

2 large eggs

1⅓ cups all-purpose flour

½ teaspoon salt

1 teaspoon baking soda

½ teaspoon baking powder

1 cup chopped walnuts

1. Preheat the oven to 350°F and grease and flour a 9" × 3" Pyrex loaf pan. Set aside.

2. Cream the butter and sugar in a large bowl. Add the banana, lemon juice, and eggs and beat until well combined. Sift in the flour, salt, baking soda, and baking powder. Beat until well combined. Stir in the walnuts.

3. Pour the batter into the prepared pan and bake in the preheated oven for 25 minutes or until a toothpick inserted in the center comes out clean. Remove from the oven and place on a rack for 10 minutes, then turn the loaf out of the pan and let it cool completely.

Makes 1 loaf.

Zucchini Bread

This zucchini bread freezes well. Just wait until it has cooled completely before wrapping it in foil and putting it in the freezer. By the way, the easiest way to grate zucchini is in a food processor.

1 cup vegetable oil
3 large eggs, beaten
2 cups sugar
2 cups grated zucchini
2 teaspoons vanilla extract
3 cups all-purpose flour, sifted
1 teaspoon baking soda
¼ teaspoon baking powder
1 teaspoon salt
3 teaspoons ground cinnamon
1 cup chopped walnuts (optional)

1. Preheat the oven to 325°F and grease two 9" × 5" × 3" loaf pans. Set aside.

2. Combine the oil, eggs, sugar, zucchini, and vanilla extract in a large bowl. Blend well.

3. Stir in the flour, baking soda, baking powder, salt, and cinnamon. DO NOT BEAT. Just mix until the dry ingredients are moistened.

4. Fold in the walnuts if you are using them. Pour the batter into the prepared loaf pans and bake in the preheated oven for 1¼ hours or until a toothpick inserted in the center comes out clean.

Makes 2 loaves.

Clemie's Cheese and Bread Casserole

My daughters' friend Clemie lives in Maine.

8 slices stale white bread, crusts removed, buttered, and torn into small pieces (Vienna bread works well)

1 1/4 pounds grated sharp Cheddar cheese

8 tablespoons margarine, melted

6 large eggs, lightly beaten

2 1/2 cups milk

1 heaping teaspoon light brown sugar

1/4 teaspoon paprika

3 finely chopped green onions

1/2 teaspoon dry mustard

1/2 teaspoon beau monde seasoning (a commercial preparation containing salt, onion powder, and celery powder)

1/2 teaspoon salt

Ground black pepper to taste

1. Preheat the oven to 375°F.

2. Grease an 8" × 11" casserole dish. Layer half the bread over the bottom of the dish, then layer half the cheese over the bread. Repeat the layers with the remaining bread and cheese. Pour the melted margarine over the top.

3. Combine the eggs, milk, brown sugar, paprika, green onions, mustard, beau monde seasoning, salt, and pepper. Pour over the bread and cheese until the liquid almost reaches the top.

4. Set the casserole dish in a pan of water and bake in the preheated oven for 40 minutes. Serve immediately.

Serves 12 people.

Luncheon and Picnic Dishes

Dieter's Soup

This soup is so delicious you should keep a container of it in your fridge at all times.

❀

Vegetable oil cooking spray
1 medium onion, chopped (about ⅓ cup)
2 cloves garlic, minced (about 1 teaspoon)
1 cup diced zucchini
1 cup diced carrot
1 tomato, diced
1 chicken bouillon cube
2 cups water
¼ teaspoon dried basil or 1 teaspoon fresh (If you have a surplus of basil in your garden, you can dry it in your microwave oven and store it in a jar in the freezer.)
¼ teaspoon ground black pepper

1. Coat a 2-quart saucepan with vegetable oil cooking spray. Add the onion and garlic and cook over a very low heat until the onion is soft. Add the zucchini, carrot, and tomato and continue cooking, covered, over a low heat for about 10 minutes. Add the bouillon cube, water, basil, and pepper and cook over a medium heat for about 10 minutes more. Remove from the heat.

2. With a slotted spoon, remove 1 cup of the cooked vegetables from the soup and put aside. Process the rest of the vegetables with the broth in a food processor until smooth.

3. Pour the puréed soup back into the saucepan. Stir in the reserved vegetables. Reheat before serving.

Serves 2 to 3 people.

Adah's Green Pea Soup

This soup is tasty hot or cold. The contents are surprising: iceberg lettuce and cream. Watch it, though. Nothing this good could be good for you.

2 cups shredded iceberg lettuce
1 10-ounce package frozen green peas
1½ cups chicken broth
⅓ cup water
¼ cup tomato juice
¼ cup finely chopped green onion
1 teaspoon minced fresh parsley
½ teaspoon salt
¼ teaspoon ground black pepper
¼ teaspoon crushed dried thyme
½ cup heavy or light cream

1. Combine all the ingredients except the cream in a 2-quart pot and bring to a boil. Reduce the heat and simmer for about 10 minutes, until the lettuce is wilted and the peas are soft. Remove from the heat.

2. Purée the soup in a blender or food processor. Just before serving, stir in the cream until well combined.

Serves 3 to 4 people.

Crab Soup

I don't worry about whether it's she-*crab soup or* he-*crab soup, whether it has the eggs in it or not. Anyway, it's illegal now to catch female crabs in the spring, when they have roe.*

It's important to cook this soup in a double boiler so that the crab flavor really comes out. And, of course, you need fresh crabmeat. This is the best, but fattening, which should be perfectly obvious, what with the cream and all.

1 pound fresh white crabmeat
3 cups milk
1 pint light cream
1½ teaspoons salt
½ teaspoon mace
⅛ teaspoon dried thyme
4 tablespoons margarine
3 tablespoons all-purpose flour
10 tablespoons sherry

1. Pick over the crabmeat carefully to make sure it contains no shell fragments or cartilage. Set aside.

2. Heat the milk, cream, salt, mace, and thyme in a medium saucepan, stirring regularly. Do not let it come to a boil.

3. While the milk-cream mixture is heating, melt the margarine in the top of a double boiler over boiling water. Add the flour and stir for a minute while it bubbles. Pour the hot milk-cream mixture over the margarine-flour mixture and stir until well combined and slightly thickened. Carefully stir in the crabmeat, being careful not to break up the flakes and lumps. Cover the top of the double

boiler and let the soup steep for 30 minutes, but do not let it come to a boil. Stir in the sherry and continue to cook, covered, for 10 minutes more. Serve in warmed soup plates.

Serves 8 people.

Shrimp Soup

The best. I do rank soups. The secret to a good shrimp soup is to cook it in a double boiler so that the flavor has a chance to come out. And be careful not to overcook the shrimp in the beginning, since you will cook it further in the soup.

1 pound fresh shrimp, cooked just until the water returns to a boil
    after the shrimp is added
5 tablespoons unsalted butter
2 ½ tablespoons all-purpose flour
½ teaspoon mace
1 teaspoon salt
½ teaspoon onion powder
Dash of garlic powder
1 teaspoon Worcestershire sauce
2 ½ cups hot milk
2 – 4 tablespoons dry sherry

1. Peel the lightly cooked shrimp and place in the bowl of a food processor. Process until the pieces of shrimp are fairly small, but do not turn the shrimp into a paste.

2. In the top of a double boiler over hot water, melt the butter. Stir in the flour with a whisk until well combined. Let the mixture bubble

for a minute, then add the mace, salt, onion powder, garlic powder, and Worcestershire sauce and stir well. Add the shrimp and stir again. Stir in the hot milk and let the soup cook in the double boiler for 5 to 7 minutes. This really brings out the flavor of the shrimp, but don't let the soup come to a boil.

3. Just before serving the soup, stir in the sherry.

Serves 4 people.

If you reheat this soup, you must use a double boiler again; otherwise it tends to curdle.

Shrimp Sandwiches

A lunchtime picnic in the backyard is one of my favorite ways of entertaining. Shrimp sandwiches are perfect for it.

1 pound cooked shrimp, peeled
3–4 tablespoons mayonnaise
1 tablespoon fresh lemon juice
2 tablespoons finely chopped onion
½ teaspoon Lawry's seasoned salt (or to taste)
½ teaspoon Dijon mustard
½ tablespoon tomato ketchup
8 slices soft white bread, crusts removed

1. Put the shrimp in the bowl of a food processor and pulse 3 or 4 times. Transfer to a bowl and stir in enough mayonnaise to make the mixture thick but spreadable. Add the lemon juice, onion, seasoned salt, mustard, and ketchup and mix until well combined.

2. Spread a thin layer of mayonnaise over 4 slices of the white bread, then spread a generous layer of the shrimp mixture. Top with the remaining slices of bread.

VARIATIONS: For some crunch, add some diced celery or jicama or whatever pleases you. Also, I sometimes serve the shrimp mixture on crackers as an hors d'oeuvre.

Makes 4 sandwiches.

Shrimp Pie

This recipe had its origins in a popular cookbook from many years ago called Make It Now, Bake It Later. *Over the many, many times I've made it, the recipe has evolved to the point that it bears only a faint resemblance to the original. For instance, I use twice as much shrimp and a lot more seasoning. But* Make It Now, Bake It Later *deserves a lot of credit for coming up with a dish that really is better for being put together at least twelve hours ahead of time. My grandson Ben LeClercq loves this pie.*

Oh, yes. Don't worry about deveining the shrimp. Once you've deveined them and then washed them again, you might as well be serving cardboard.

2 pounds raw shrimp, heads removed
2 cups light cream
1 teaspoon dry mustard
1 teaspoon salt
1 tablespoon Worcestershire sauce

½ teaspoon mace

3 large eggs

6–8 slices white bread, crusts removed and torn into pieces

1 8-ounce package Olde English cheese slices, torn into pieces (Cheddar cheese may be substituted)

8 tablespoons unsalted butter or margarine, melted

1. Cook the shrimp in boiling, salted water, drain, rinse under cold running water, peel, and set aside.

2. In a blender, combine the cream, mustard, salt, Worcestershire sauce, mace, and eggs. Set aside.

3. Layer half the bread pieces over the bottom of a greased 2-quart casserole dish, followed by a layer of half the shrimp. Sprinkle half the cheese over the shrimp. Repeat the bread, shrimp, and cheese layers. Pour the melted butter or margarine over the pie, followed by the cream-egg mixture. Cover the casserole dish and refrigerate overnight.

4. The next day, remove the casserole dish from the refrigerator and let it sit at room temperature for an hour. Preheat the oven to 350°F.

5. Cook the shrimp pie, covered, for 1 hour in the preheated oven. Serve immediately.

Serves 4 to 6 people.

Crab and Shrimp Over English Muffins

Serve this with a green salad for a very elegant lunch.

3 tablespoons unsalted butter
2 cups sliced mushrooms
2 ribs celery, sliced thin
1 10¾-ounce can Cheddar cheese soup
1 5-ounce jar Cheddar cheese spread
1 pound crabmeat
1 pound cooked shrimp, peeled
6 English muffins

1. Melt the butter in a large sauté pan and add the mushrooms and celery. Cook over a medium-high heat, stirring occasionally, until all the moisture has evaporated and the celery is soft.

2. Add the soup and cheese spread, reduce the heat to medium-low, and cook until well heated but not boiling, stirring constantly.

3. Stir in the crabmeat and shrimp and let the mixture gently simmer for a few minutes while you split and toast the English muffins. Spoon the mixture over the crisp muffins and serve immediately.

Serves 6 people.

Crab Quiche

Strong men pretend they don't eat quiche, but of course there's nothing made with crab that isn't a treat to eat. There is this about crab, however: A good many people are allergic to it. I never serve it that I don't ask, ahead of time, "Can you eat crab?"

For this quiche, you can use a store-bought pie crust or make your own using my recipe for pâte brisée (see page 217).

1 9" pie crust
½ cup mayonnaise
2 tablespoons all-purpose flour
2 large eggs, well beaten
½ cup milk
⅛ teaspoon mace
2 cups grated Swiss cheese
2 tablespoons margarine
½ cup chopped green onion
8 ounces crabmeat
Paprika for sprinkling

1. Preheat the oven to 400°F.

2. Press heavy-duty aluminum foil over the unfilled pie crust and prebake it for 30 minutes in the preheated oven. (The foil will keep the unfilled crust from puffing up.) Remove the crust from the oven, take off the foil, and set aside to cool.

3. Reduce the oven temperature to 350°F.

4. With an electric mixer, combine the mayonnaise, flour, eggs, milk, mace, and 1 cup of the Swiss cheese. Set aside.

5. In a small skillet, melt the margarine over medium-low heat. Add the green onion and sauté until soft, but do not brown. Remove from the heat.

6. Fold the green onion and crabmeat gently into the mayonnaise mixture, being careful not to break up the crab flakes and lumps. Pour the filling into the prebaked pie shell and sprinkle the remaining Swiss cheese over the top. Sprinkle the quiche with paprika.

7. Bake in the 350°F oven for 30 to 35 minutes, until the quiche is set and golden brown on top. The quiche should rest for about 10 minutes before serving.

Serves 4 to 6 people.

The quiche can be cooked ahead of time and reheated before serving.

Chicken and Biscuits

A success every time. Put in sautéed mushrooms and anything else that strikes your fancy. Make sure the gravy covers the chicken completely and don't forget the layer of biscuits on top. An old recipe and one that can easily be cut in half.

10 chicken breast halves
12 tablespoons unsalted butter
1 large Vidalia onion, sliced
¾ cup all-purpose flour
6 cups chicken broth
Juice of 1 lemon
½ teaspoon garlic powder

½ teaspoon dried thyme

1 tablespoon sugar

Lawry's seasoned salt to taste

1 chicken bouillon cube (optional)

4 hard-boiled eggs, sliced (optional)

1 8-ounce can sliced water chestnuts (optional)

1 pound mushrooms, sliced and sautéed in 4 tablespoons unsalted butter (optional)

12 unbaked buttermilk biscuits, homemade or store-bought

1. Preheat the oven to 425°F.

2. Place the chicken breasts in a slow cooker. Do not add any liquid. Cook until tender. If you do not have a slow cooker, place the chicken breasts in a large, deep pot, add a few inches of water, and bring to a boil. Reduce the heat and let the breasts simmer for about 20 minutes. When the chicken has cooked, remove it from the slow cooker or pot, allow to cool, then tear into bite-size pieces, discarding the bones. Put the chicken pieces into an 8" × 11" × 3" casserole dish or divide between two smaller ones. Set aside.

3. In a large saucepan or frying pan, melt the butter. Sauté the onion slices until they are translucent. Do not brown. Add the flour and stir as it begins to bubble. Add the chicken broth, stirring constantly until the gravy thickens. Stir in the lemon juice, garlic powder, thyme, sugar, and seasoned salt. If you want the gravy to have a strong chicken taste, add the bouillon cube. You can also add the hard-boiled eggs, water chestnuts, and mushrooms at this point. I particularly like the eggs and mushrooms.

4. Pour the gravy over the chicken pieces. Everything in the casserole must be covered. Place the biscuits on top of the gravy in a circle.

Place in the preheated oven. After about 12 minutes, check the casserole: The biscuits should be brown. Reduce the oven temperature to 300°F and cook the chicken and biscuits for 40 to 45 minutes more. If the biscuits start to get too brown, cover them lightly with foil and continue to bake. Serve hot from the oven.

Serves 8 people.

Chicken Salad

This is a tasty lunch dish. If you have leftovers, they can be used as a quiche filling. Or chop the leftovers a little finer in a food processor, add some milk, and they make a good soup. Using chicken tenders for this recipe is a real plus. Not only do they save time, but they are white meat and the most tender part of the chicken.

3 tablespoons unsalted butter
1½ pounds chicken tenders
½ cup mayonnaise
1 teaspoon Worcestershire sauce
1 teaspoon Dijon mustard
1 teaspoon salt
2 hard-boiled eggs, chopped
½ cup chopped celery
1 tablespoon finely diced onion
½ cup sliced stuffed green olives
1 tablespoon capers
⅛ teaspoon garlic powder
2 tablespoons fresh lemon juice

1. Melt the butter in a frying pan over low heat and cook the chicken tenders in it for 5 to 7 minutes. Alternately, you can cook the tenders for a few minutes on high in a microwave. Cut a chicken tender in half to make sure they are done. They should be tender but there should be no pink. Cut all the tenders into bite-size pieces.

2. In a large bowl, thoroughly mix the mayonnaise, Worcestershire sauce, mustard, and salt. Fold in the eggs, celery, onion, olives, capers, garlic powder, lemon juice, and chicken. If you are not going to serve it immediately, refrigerate in a covered bowl.

Serves 6 people.

Margaret's Fried Chicken

I can't fry chicken and I don't try. My cook Margaret's is the best I've ever eaten.

1 fryer, cut into pieces
Salt and ground black pepper to taste
1 teaspoon onion powder
1 teaspoon garlic powder
2 large eggs
1 cup milk
1 cup self-rising flour
1 quart corn or vegetable oil

1. Wash the chicken and pat dry with paper towels. Rub with the salt, pepper, onion powder, and garlic powder. Refrigerate the chicken in a covered bowl overnight.

2. The next day, remove the chicken from the refrigerator and pour off any liquid that has accumulated in the bowl. With an electric mixer, beat the eggs and milk in a large bowl. Put the flour in a strong, good-size paper bag. Dip each piece of chicken in the egg-milk mixture, coating thoroughly. Put the coated chicken, a few pieces at a time, in the paper bag with the flour and shake. Remove the chicken from the bag, shake off any excess flour, and place on a plate.

3. Heat the oil in a Dutch oven or other large pot suitable for deep-frying. When the oil begins to simmer and pop (about 350°F on a frying thermometer), add the chicken, a few pieces at a time. You want to maintain the temperature of the oil so that the chicken will cook slowly. If the oil gets much hotter, the chicken will be cooked on the outside but not near the bone. Each batch of chicken should take about 15 minutes to cook through. Drain the fried chicken on paper towels. If you are not going to serve it immediately, you can put it on a baking sheet in a 150°F oven, but keep your eye on it. The chicken is also very good served at room temperature.

Serves 4 people.

Chedda Cheese Soufflé

This soufflé can be assembled and refrigerated for two hours until you are ready to bake it. Eat it the minute it comes out of the oven.

2 tablespoons fine, dry bread crumbs

3 tablespoons unsalted butter

2 tablespoons minced onion

3 tablespoons all-purpose flour

1 cup milk

3 tablespoons stone-ground horseradish mustard

Dash of salt and ground black pepper

¾ cup grated Cheddar cheese

4 large eggs, separated, plus 1 additional egg white

1. Preheat the oven to 375°F.

2. Butter a 6-cup soufflé dish and sprinkle the bottom and sides with the bread crumbs.

3. In a large skillet, melt the butter and sauté the onion over medium heat until soft, but do not brown. Stir in the flour. With a whisk or wooden spoon, gradually stir in the milk. Add the mustard, salt, and pepper and stir until the mixture has thickened. Stir in the cheese and the 4 egg yolks and continue cooking until the cheese has melted. Remove from the heat and set aside.

4. In a large bowl, beat the 5 egg whites until they form stiff, but not dry, peaks. Fold a quarter of them into the cheese mixture. Gently fold the cheese mixture into the remaining egg whites. Pour into the prepared soufflé dish.

5. Bake in the preheated oven for 20 to 25 minutes. Serve immediately.

Serves 6 people.

Margaret's Macaroni Pie

This version of macaroni and cheese is really more of a custard. Make sure the egg-milk mixture covers the macaroni completely or you'll have dry noodles on top. It is my cook Margaret's recipe, and what makes it worth eating is the cheese. My grandsons rank it with her fried chicken.

8 ounces uncooked macaroni
10 ounces grated extra-sharp Cheddar cheese
4 tablespoons margarine, melted
2 large eggs
1 teaspoon Dijon mustard
2 cups milk

1. Preheat the oven to 350°F.

2. Cook the macaroni in boiling, salted water until just tender. Drain and return to the pot. While the macaroni is still hot, stir in half of the cheese and all of the melted margarine. Transfer the mixture to a 1½-quart casserole dish.

3. In a medium bowl, beat together the eggs, mustard, and milk. Pour over the macaroni and bake in the preheated oven for 20 minutes. Remove the casserole from the oven, sprinkle the remaining cheese over the top, and return it to the oven for 10 minutes more. Serve immediately.

Serves 4 people.

Many People's Eggplant Pie

I thought this was Miss Em's recipe, but she says my sister, Peach, and I made it up out at Fox Bank. Whoever first created it, it's a good one, and it's still delicious when served the next day.

1 good size eggplant (about 1½ pounds), peeled and
    cut into 1" cubes
1½ tablespoons margarine
1 large onion, sliced
1 green pepper, sliced
1 tablespoon all purpose flour
1 tablespoon light brown sugar
1 14½-ounce can tomatoes, with the juice
½ teaspoon salt
3 slices several-day-old white bread
3 tablespoons unsalted butter

1. Preheat the oven to 350°F.

2. Cook the eggplant cubes in boiling, salted water until tender, about 4 minutes. Drain and set aside.

3. Melt the margarine in a large skillet and sauté the onion and green pepper until soft, but do not brown. Add the flour and let bubble for a minute while stirring. Add the brown sugar and stir, then the tomatoes and salt. Let the mixture simmer for a couple of minutes until it thickens a bit. Add the eggplant cubes and bring back to a boil. Transfer the mixture to a casserole dish.

4. Tear the bread slices into pieces and pulse in a food processor until they are crumbs. Melt the butter in a small skillet and stir in the

bread crumbs until they are well coated with butter. Sprinkle the crumbs over the eggplant mixture.

5. Bake in the preheated oven for 30 minutes. Serve piping hot.

VARIATION: You can serve this dish without baking it and it still tastes awfully good. Just omit the buttered bread crumbs.

Serves 8 people.

Corn Pie

It's a treat — delicious — and frozen corn can be used out of season.

8 ears fresh corn, preferably Silver Queen
3 tablespoons unsalted butter
1 tablespoon all-purpose flour
1 teaspoon salt
2 tablespoons sugar
1 cup light cream
3 large eggs, well beaten

1. Preheat the oven to 350°F.

2. Cut the kernels off the cob with a sharp knife; you will have about 1 cup of corn with its milk. Set aside.

3. Melt the butter in a medium saucepan. Add the flour and stir or whisk for a minute, then add the salt, sugar, and light cream, combining thoroughly. Using a whisk, slowly add the eggs, being careful not to let the mixture come to a boil. Remove from the heat and stir in the corn kernels. Pour the mixture into a greased casserole dish.

4. Place the casserole dish in a pan of hot water that is large enough for the water to come halfway up the side of the casserole. Carefully place in the preheated oven and bake for 35 to 45 minutes. The pie is done when a knife inserted in the middle comes out clean. Serve immediately.

Serves 6 people.

Tomato and Onion Tart

Marty and Miss Em found the recipe for this tart in Gourmet *magazine and serve it all the time for anybody who turns up. It's like a grown-up's pizza. I think it should be served just off of hot, though they think it's equally good at room temperature. All of us have tinkered with it.*

The buttery pastry for this tart can be used for any number of savory pies, and if you want to use it for a sweet one, just cut back on the salt to a half teaspoon. The dough can also be made three days ahead and chilled until you're ready to use it or it can be frozen for up to a month.

PASTRY:

2 cups all-purpose flour

1½ teaspoons salt

12 tablespoons unsalted butter, chilled and cut into 12 pieces

6—7 tablespoons ice water

FILLING:

2 tablespoons olive oil

2 large onions, sliced thin

Dijon mustard to taste

½ pound grated Jack or Gruyère cheese

1 pound plum tomatoes or ½ pound plum and ½ pound yellow tomatoes, cut into ½" wedges

¼ cup pitted Niçoise olives

Salt and ground black pepper to taste

1. To make the tart pastry, sift the flour and salt into a large, chilled bowl. With a pastry blender or your fingertips, lightly blend in the butter until the mixture resembles coarse meal. Add 1 tablespoon of ice water at a time, tossing lightly with a fork until the mixture begins to form a dough.

2. On a lightly floured surface, gently knead the dough 3 or 4 times. Form the dough into a ball and then flatten it to form a disk. Wrap the disk in plastic wrap and place in the refrigerator for an hour.

3. While the dough is chilling, preheat the oven to 375°F and make the tart filling. In a large skillet, heat the olive oil and cook the onions, covered, until soft, stirring occasionally. Remove the cover and continue to cook the onions until they are golden and any liquid has evaporated. Remove from the heat.

4. Remove the dough from the refrigerator and let it sit at room temperature for 10 minutes to make it easier to roll out. On a lightly floured surface, using a lightly floured rolling pin, roll out the dough to form a 14" circle about ⅛" thick. Gently transfer the dough to a 12" tart pan with a removable, fluted rim. Spread Dijon mustard over dough. Spread the onions over the bottom of the crust and top with the cheese. Arrange the tomato wedges and olives in concentric circles on top of the cheese and season to taste with salt and pepper.

5. Bake the tart in the middle of the preheated oven for about 45 minutes, until the pastry is golden. Cool a bit on a rack before removing the fluted rim. Serve warm or at room temperature.

Serves 8 people.

My Biscuits

This is my own special recipe that I've had for a long time, but I should confess to you that there's a frozen buttermilk biscuit out there that's hard to beat.

2 cups self-rising flour
2 tablespoons sugar
8 tablespoons unsalted butter or margarine, chilled and cut
  into 8 pieces
¾ cup milk

1. Preheat the oven to 425°F.

2. In a large bowl, sift together the flour and sugar. Cut in the butter or margarine until the mixture is the consistency of coarse cornmeal. With a fork, mix in ½ cup of the milk. Continue adding milk in small amounts until the dough is soft but not sticky. You may not need the full ¾ cup milk.

3. On a lightly floured surface, with a lightly floured rolling pin, roll out the dough to ½" thickness. Cut out the biscuits with a biscuit cutter or sharp knife and place on an ungreased baking sheet. Bake in the preheated oven for 10 to 12 minutes. Serve directly from the oven with plenty of butter.

Makes about 12 biscuits.

You can make your own self-rising flour. Just add 1½ teaspoons baking powder and ½ teaspoon salt to every cup of flour.

Cocktail Snacks and Condiments

Pat's Crab Canapés

This recipe is so easy to prepare and it freezes well, so you can always have something delicious ready to go for unexpected guests.

1 5-ounce jar sharp Cheddar cheese spread
1½ tablespoons mayonnaise
½ teaspoon Lawry's seasoned salt
8 tablespoons unsalted butter
1 pound white crabmeat
6 English muffins

1. In the top of a double boiler over hot water, stir the cheese spread, mayonnaise, seasoned salt, and butter until well combined and soft enough to spread. Remove the top of the double boiler from the heat and carefully fold the crabmeat into the warm mixture.

2. Split open the English muffins, place them on an ungreased baking sheet, and spread some of the crabmeat mixture over the top of each muffin half. Cut each muffin half into 6 wedges. If you are not going to serve them immediately, cover the baking sheet with plastic wrap and place in the freezer until ready to use.

3. For canapés that have not been frozen, place under the broiler for several minutes, until lightly browned on top. If they have been frozen, place *unthawed* under the broiler for 5 to 7 minutes. Serve piping hot (they are not good when cold).

Makes 72 canapés.

Artichoke Canapés

Lots of taste and not so much mayonnaise. The recipe can also be made with canned artichoke hearts, in which case the hearts do not need to be cooked first, only drained.

1 9-ounce package frozen artichoke hearts
½ cup mayonnaise
½ cup grated Parmesan cheese
1 clove garlic, minced, or ⅛ teaspoon garlic powder

1. Preheat the oven to 350°F.

2. Place the frozen artichoke hearts in a saucepan with a tablespoon of water. Bring to a boil; cover and cook for about 3 minutes, making sure the water does not evaporate (add a little more water if it gets low). Uncover the saucepan and separate the artichoke hearts with a fork. Cook uncovered for about 2 minutes, until soft. Remove from the heat and drain well.

3. Process the artichoke hearts in a food processor until finely minced. Add the mayonnaise, cheese, and garlic and process until well mixed.

4. Transfer the artichoke mixture to a small gratin dish and bake uncovered in the preheated oven until it bubbles and is lightly browned on top, about 20 minutes. Serve warm on crackers.

Makes enough for about 15 canapés.

Broiled Oysters Wrapped in Bacon

As you probably know, oysters are eaten only in the months that have an r *in them—that is,* not *in May, June, July, or August. Fall's the best time for clams and oysters, I think.*

Shucked oysters
Uncooked bacon strips

Wrap each oyster in a third of a strip of bacon and secure with a toothpick. Put under the broiler for 2 or 3 minutes, turning them once while they cook. They are ready when the bacon is browned and the oysters' edges have curled.

Vegetable Pickles

In the old days in South Carolina, a dining table without a bowl of either artichoke or green tomato pickles was incomplete. Every home had a commodious storeroom with lots of shelves holding row upon row of pickles and preserves. There were always several families whose pickles were considered so good that the recipe was a closely guarded secret. I once knew a man who, when tense and strung out, would relax by making pickles and canning them. It was a day's job and, of course, the relaxing was helped along by sips of icy cold gin and tonics. If he'd been my husband and I had to deal with the kitchen after he'd completed all this relaxing, his tenseness and strung-outness would have been just beginning. So let me warn you: Making and canning pickles is no joke. It takes time and it's hot work and it requires the proper equipment and storage space.

In this recipe, it's the pickling solution that's the secret to success. The recipe can be used with a great variety of vegetables.

8 cucumbers, sliced (Jerusalem artichokes can be substituted)
2 quarts sliced onion
4 green peppers, sliced
1 head cauliflower, cut up
1 cup pickling salt

PICKLING SOLUTION:
4 cups sugar
4 cups cider vinegar
¾ cup all-purpose flour
¼ cup dry mustard
1½ tablespoons ground turmeric
½ teaspoon ground cinnamon
1 tablespoon celery seed

1. Combine the vegetables and pickling salt in a large bowl, cover with water, and let stand overnight.

2. Drain the vegetables, but do not rinse them. Set aside.

3. In a large pot, bring the sugar and vinegar to a boil, stirring until the sugar dissolves.

4. In a small bowl, combine the flour and mustard with just enough of the sugar-vinegar mixture from the pot to make a thin paste. Stir the paste into the boiling sugar-vinegar mixture along with the turmeric, cinnamon, and celery seed. Boil for a couple of minutes, stirring constantly.

5. Carefully spoon the drained vegetables into the boiling pickling solution and stir. Return to a boil and cook for a minute. Remove from the heat. Ladle the vegetables and pickling solution into sterile jars, seal, and process for 20 minutes in a boiling-water bath. Store the jars in a cool, dark place.

Makes 4 quarts.

Mary and Anne's Chutney

Mary and Anne made this chutney in Flat Rock. It's a secret where they got their peaches—but in South Carolina somewhere. We'd ask, "Can we go and get some peaches, too?" Oh, no. They'd bring us each three or four peaches for our own use. Then they'd get in Mary's antiquated kitchen. You never saw such. No gadgets in that kitchen. Just boiling pots. They'd come out with perfectly wonderful chutney. They'd give jars away for Christmas. Tiny, tiny, little jars. I knew Mary would never give me that recipe. She died, sad to say, and I thought it wouldn't do to lose that recipe. Anne gave it to me.

One thing about a chutney: You must make sure the syrup is thick enough. Some fruits have more juice than others, so it's a judgment call when cooking. This chutney adds a delicious extra to all meats and chicken and is even an excellent hors d'oeuvre when served with cream cheese on crackers.

❦

2 ½ cups sugar
3 cups white distilled vinegar
½ pound fresh ginger, peeled and cut into ⅛" × 1" strips
1 pound peaches or pears, peeled and cut into ½" chunks

2 mangoes (about 1 pound), peeled and cut into ½" chunks
½ tablespoon chili powder
1 tablespoon mustard seed
1 clove garlic, sliced
¾ cup raisins

1. In a large saucepan, combine 1¼ cups of the sugar, 1½ cups of the vinegar, and the ginger strips. Bring to a boil and cook until the mixture is a thick syrup, about 20 minutes. Remove from the heat and set aside.

2. In a large pot, combine the remaining 1¼ cups sugar and 1½ cups vinegar, along with the chunks of fruit. Bring to a boil and cook for about 20 minutes, until the liquid is a thick syrup. Remove from the heat. With a slotted spoon, remove the fruit to a bowl and set aside. Pour the syrup remaining in the pot into the saucepan with the ginger syrup. Boil for 5 minutes, stirring to combine the syrups.

3. To the combined syrups, add the chili powder, mustard seed, garlic, raisins, and reserved fruit. Boil for about 30 minutes more, stirring occasionally, until the syrup is quite thick.

4. Divide the chutney between 2 sterile pint jars, seal, and process for 15 minutes in a boiling-water bath. Store the jars in a cool, dark place.

Makes about 2 pints.

Hot Fruit Curry

This is an especially good side dish with meats like venison and pork.

1 medium can sliced pears, drained
2 medium cans sliced peaches, drained
2 medium cans pineapple chunks, drained
2 medium cans sour cherries, drained
2 medium cans apricots, drained
1 medium can white grapes, drained
1 cup dark brown sugar
3 tablespoons all-purpose flour
1 tablespoon curry powder
16 tablespoons unsalted butter, cut into pea-size pieces

1. Preheat the oven to 350°F.

2. Combine all the drained fruits and spoon into a large, shallow casserole dish.

3. Combine the brown sugar, flour, and curry powder and stir into the fruit. Dot with the butter and bake in the preheated oven for ½ hour. Serve immediately.

VARIATION: If you like crunchiness, stir some granola cereal into the fruit along with the sugar mixture.
Serves 10 people.

Fig Preserves

Fig preserves are so Southern. Every little community down here made them when the little sugar figs were ripe. If you didn't make them yourself, you could always count on finding some for sale at the Christmas church bazaars. By the way, do not mash the figs. It's not jam you're making here, it's preserves.

These preserves are delicious on toast for breakfast, but a special treat when spooned over vanilla ice cream.

2 pounds fresh figs
Juice of 1 lemon
2 pounds sugar
1 lemon, sliced thin

1. Wash the figs and set aside.

2. In a large pot, bring the lemon juice and sugar to a boil, stirring regularly. Drop in the figs and sliced lemon and return to a boil over medium heat. Cook for ½ hour, stirring regularly. Remove from the heat.

3. With a slotted spoon, remove the figs and lemon slices to a bowl. Return the syrup to the stove, bring to a hard boil, and cook for about 20 minutes, stirring occasionally, until thickened. Drop the figs and lemon slices back into the syrup, return to a boil, and cook for ½ hour more. Remove from the heat.

4. Spoon the hot preserves into sterile jars, seal, and store in a cool, dark place.

Makes about 2 pints.

Dinner Dishes

—◆—

including

6 Recipes for Wild Fish

and Game

Crab Casserole or Ramekins

A ramekin is a little individual baking dish, in this case an open shell, a seashell of your choosing—a scallop shell or even the crab back itself. When I use scallop shells as ramekins, I add a few cooked shrimp to the recipe.

4 tablespoons unsalted butter
1 cup bread crumbs or cornflake crumbs
1 teaspoon salt
½ teaspoon dried tarragon or 1½ teaspoons fresh
1 teaspoon Worcestershire sauce
1 teaspoon prepared mustard
1 heaping tablespoon mayonnaise
1 tablespoon tomato ketchup
1 cup milk
2 tablespoons margarine
1½ tablespoons all-purpose flour
1 egg yolk
1 pound crabmeat

1. Preheat the oven to 375°F.

2. Melt the butter in a medium skillet. Add the bread crumbs and stir until coated with butter. Remove from the heat and set aside.

3. Mix the salt, tarragon, Worcestershire sauce, mustard, mayonnaise, and ketchup into the milk mixture in a small bowl. Set aside.

4. Melt the margarine in a large skillet and stir in the flour. Let bubble a minute. Pour the milk mixture into the skillet and stir until thickened. Turn off the heat and add the egg yolk.

5. Fold the crabmeat into the cream sauce very gently, so as not to break up the crab flakes and lumps. Spoon this mixture into a medium casserole dish or into 6 or 7 carefully cleaned crab or scallop shells. Sprinkle the buttered bread crumbs over the mixture.

6. Bake in the preheated oven until the casserole is bubbling and browned, about 12 to 15 minutes. Serve immediately.

Serves 6 or 7 people as an appetizer.

Oysters on the Half Shell

I love fried oysters but am not much on raw ones. For Ben and his brother, though, they were the oil that greased the wheels of life. When Ben retired and was very old, eating seafood was one of his main enjoyments. Mel Lofton, from up the coast, was my gardener then and he worked part-time on the water as well. He taught me a great deal about gardening and he also taught me to keep a half bushel of oysters in my freezer at all times. When you want some to eat, just take out however many you need. While still frozen, put them in a pan with a couple of tablespoons of water and pop them in a preheated 425°F oven. Watch them closely. In a few minutes, the shells will open just a crack. Take them out of the oven immediately, slip a knife in that small crack, twist the knife, and you're in business. The oysters will still be cold and deliciously salty.

Scalloped Oysters

The first time I tasted this dish, I asked what was in it. It's full of cream. I said, "What?" I should have known. I was refusing to understand. I believe the cream was already clogging the arteries leading to my brain. Mr. Burbage, whose grocery is a Charleston institution, gets credit for this treat.

24 saltine crackers
8 tablespoons unsalted butter
1 pint shucked oysters, drained (reserve the liquor)
Salt and ground black pepper to taste
1 large egg, well beaten
½ cup light cream or milk

1. Preheat the oven to 375°F.

2. Turn the saltines into crumbs in a food processor or with a rolling pin. Melt the butter in a large skillet and stir in the cracker crumbs, coating them thoroughly with butter. Do not brown them, though. Remove from the heat.

3. Layer a third of the cracker crumbs over the bottom of a deep 1-quart casserole dish. Layer half the oysters over the crumbs. Sprinkle with salt and pepper. Layer another third of the crumbs over the oysters, then layer the remaining oysters over them. Sprinkle again with salt and pepper.

4. Mix the reserved oyster liquor with the egg and cream or milk and pour over the top of the casserole. Top with the remaining third of the cracker crumbs. Bake in the preheated oven until it bubbles, about 20 minutes. Do not overcook or the oysters will be tough. Serve hot from the oven.

Serves 4 people.

Pawleys Island Crab Cakes

Pawleys Island is an old resort beach about sixty miles north of Charleston. Its beach is the best anywhere. That beautiful clear water and you get in deep so quickly—it has the proper slope for a beach.

I should mention that these crab cakes are a perfect take-along gift for any hostess. Telephone ahead and say, "I'm going to bring you a dozen crab cakes for the first evening we're there. I don't want you to have to do any work on that first evening." Just call a week ahead.

The crab cake mixture is very soft. For the first coating of bread crumbs, simply put a generous amount of crumbs right in your hands along with a patty. After the patties have been refrigerated for an hour, they can be rolled on a plate for the second coating of bread crumbs.

1 cup mayonnaise
1½ tablespoons extra-fine cracker crumbs
Large pinch of cayenne pepper
⅛ teaspoon ground celery seed
⅛ teaspoon dry mustard
¼ teaspoon fresh lemon juice
1 egg white
1 pound fresh lump crabmeat
1¼ cups fine, dry bread crumbs
6 tablespoons unsalted butter
Lemon wedges for garnish

1. In a large bowl, thoroughly blend the mayonnaise, cracker crumbs, cayenne pepper, celery seed, mustard, lemon juice, and egg white. Gently fold the crabmeat into the mixture, taking care not to break up the lumps.

2. Divide the mixture into 6 equal portions, form each portion into a patty, and gently roll the patties in half of the bread crumbs right in your hands, one at a time. Refrigerate the patties for 1 hour, then gently roll them in the remaining bread crumbs before frying them.

3. Melt the butter in a heavy 10" skillet over medium-low heat. Place the crab cakes in the skillet and cook 2 minutes on each side, taking care not to burn them. Drain the cakes on paper towels, transfer them to a heated platter, and serve immediately with the lemon wedges.

Serves 6 people as an appetizer, 3 as a main course.

Paella

This tasty paella recipe cooks on top of the stove and in one pan, which makes it easy to prepare and serve. If you have a good-looking paellero— a traditional paella pan—the sky's the limit! If you don't have one, just use a large skillet with a tight-fitting lid.

5 tablespoons olive oil
1 cup sliced onion
1 cup sliced green pepper
½ cup sliced sweet red pepper
1 cup sliced celery
2 cups raw rice
4 cups chicken broth
¼ teaspoon saffron

1 boneless, skinless chicken breast, cut into 1"-wide strips
2 cups 1"-wide strips cooked ham
3 hot or sweet Italian sausages, cooked and cut into 1" pieces
½ pound cooked shrimp, peeled (optional)

1. Heat 3 tablespoons of the olive oil in a paellero or large skillet and sauté the onion, green pepper, red pepper, and celery just until soft.

2. Stir in the rice, followed by the chicken broth and saffron. Bring to a hard boil, stir, and continue boiling for 5 minutes. Turn the heat down to low, cover the paellero, and let the mixture cook until the rice is tender, about 15 minutes. If the rice is not yet tender and there is little or no broth left in the paellero, add a little water and continue cooking until the rice is done.

3. While the rice is cooking, heat 2 tablespoons of olive oil in a small skillet and lightly brown the chicken strips. When the rice is tender, add the chicken, ham, and sausage to the paellero. Cook for 10 minutes, stirring frequently. If you are using shrimp, stir them into the paella and cook it just long enough to heat the shrimp, about 2 to 3 minutes. Serve immediately.

VARIATION: Once I added 2 cups of sliced zucchini and yellow squash about 5 minutes before the rice had finished cooking. The vegetables were steamed just enough at the end and they made the paella a complete meal in itself.

Serves 4 people.

Webb's Chicken

A Sunday roaster cooked like this is delectable! I usually serve it with small new potatoes, which can be added to the roasting pan about halfway through the cooking time.

❇

1 large roaster (5–7 pounds)
Vegetable oil for coating
Salt and ground black pepper to taste
3 medium onions, quartered
3 oranges, unpeeled and quartered
½ cup honey
½ cup orange juice

1. Preheat the oven to 400°F.

2. Lightly coat the outside of the roaster with vegetable oil, then salt and pepper both the inside and outside of the chicken. Place in a shallow roasting pan.

3. Stuff the roaster with a quartered onion and a quartered orange. Place the remaining onion and orange quarters around the roaster.

4. To make the basting mixture, heat the honey and orange juice in a small saucepan; if you don't heat this mixture, it will not combine. Set aside.

5. Place the roaster in the preheated oven. After 15 minutes, reduce the heat to 350°F and begin basting every 10 to 15 minutes with the honey–orange juice mixture. Roast the chicken for about 2 hours or until the juices run clear.

Serves 6 to 8 people.

Priscilla's Chicken

*You can sit on the porch and have a drink while this one's in the oven.
I think the original recipe may have come off the back of a Bisquick box.
We've improved it. It's remarkably crisp, like good fried chicken but made
with scarcely any fat.*

²⁄₃ cup Bisquick
1½ teaspoons paprika
1¼ teaspoons salt
1¼ teaspoons ground black pepper
½ teaspoon onion powder
¼ teaspoon garlic powder
1 fryer (2½–3 pounds), cut into pieces
1 tablespoon margarine, melted

GRAVY (OPTIONAL):
Drippings from chicken
1 tablespoon all-purpose flour
1 cup chicken broth

1. Preheat the oven to 425°F.

2. Put the Bisquick, paprika, salt, pepper, onion powder, and garlic
   powder in a paper bag. Add the chicken pieces and shake the bag
   until the chicken is well coated.

3. Coat the bottom of a 13" × 9" baking pan with the melted
   margarine. Place the chicken pieces skin side down in the pan,
   making sure they do not touch one another. Place in the preheated
   oven and bake for 35 minutes. Turn the chicken pieces over and
   bake 15 to 20 minutes more.

4. Remove the chicken from the baking pan and, if you want to make gravy, put the pan on a burner over medium heat. Add the flour to the pan drippings with a whisk and cook for about a minute, until the drippings and flour are well combined. Add the broth and continue whisking for a few minutes more, until the gravy has thickened. Serve warm in a gravy boat, alongside the chicken.

Serves 4 people.

The Marinated Chicken Breasts I Like

These chicken breasts can easily become an hors d'oeuvre for a cocktail party. Just cut the breasts into strips before marinating them. When they've cooked, serve with toothpicks.

6 skinless, boneless chicken breast halves
⅓ cup Dijon mustard
¼ cup white wine
1 tablespoon honey
2 cups fine bread crumbs
1 cup finely grated extra-sharp Cheddar cheese

1. Preheat the oven to 500°F.

2. Flatten each chicken breast half with the bottom of a small, heavy frying pan or with a meat pounder.

3. For the marinade, put the mustard, wine, and honey in a large resealable plastic bag. Add the chicken breasts, seal the bag, and marinate in the refrigerator for an hour.

4. In a medium bowl, thoroughly mix the bread crumbs and grated cheese. Dip the marinated chicken breasts in this mixture, coating all sides.

5. Place the chicken breasts in a greased baking pan and cook in the preheated oven for 10 to 12 minutes. If you won't be serving them immediately, turn off the oven and leave the door cracked open a bit.

Serves 6 people.

Louisa's Ginger Chicken

This chicken is very tender, very tasty, and very popular, but you must dress it the night before, so plan ahead. It's not the easiest to cook. You have to stay home to make this one.

1 good-size fryer (3–3½ pounds)
Salt to taste
2½ cups water
1 large onion, sliced
2 cloves garlic, sliced
2 teaspoons ground ginger
Juice of 1 lemon
2 tablespoons unsalted butter

1. Butterfly the fryer, saving the wing tips, neck, and giblets in the refrigerator for the basting stock. If you do not know how to butterfly poultry or do not have the equipment to do it, ask your butcher, but make sure he gives you the parts you'll need for the stock.

2. Place the fryer on a large plate, salt it to taste, cover it loosely with aluminum foil, and place in the refrigerator overnight.

3. The next day, prepare the basting stock about an hour before you plan to start cooking the chicken. Put the water, onion, garlic, and reserved chicken parts in a large pot and bring to a boil. Reduce the heat and let the stock simmer for the next hour or so.

4. Preheat the oven to 425°F.

5. Remove the chicken from the refrigerator. Rub it all over with the ground ginger, drizzle the lemon juice over it, and dot with the butter. Put it skin side down in a roasting pan and cook in the preheated oven for 15 to 20 minutes. The skin will brown nicely.

6. While the chicken is browning, remove the stock from the stove and strain it. Remove the chicken from the oven and turn it skin side up. Reduce the oven temperature to 325°F, put the chicken back in the oven, and baste it with the stock every 20 minutes or so over the course of the next 1½ hours. If you use up the stock, baste the chicken with the pan drippings. Carve the chicken and serve it hot or cold.

Serves 4 people.

Fresh Beef Brisket

Real brisket is a hard cut to get. We had what was called a beef club when I was growing up in Pinopolis. There was no refrigeration in the village, so a cow was butchered every two weeks and divided by the families that "subscribed." A man came driving a mule and wagon with the meat in an old "safe"—a screened-in box—on the back. Well, when he got inside our gate, every hound in the yard would gather round. Each got a tidbit. Cousin Deas Porcher always wanted and got the brisket and she could cook it deliciously. In fact, my whole idea of "delicious" back then was a slice of loaf bread with gravy from the brisket on it. But I didn't think about brisket again for years until I tasted it at my friend Louisa's. You just wrap the whole thing up like a Christmas package. And there's no tending. A cocktail-party treat. Men who claim they want only those rare morsels will crowd around the brisket. Tender and delicious. But be warned: You can't always get brisket, at least not in Charleston.

2 ½ – 3 ½ pounds beef brisket
2 envelopes onion soup mix

1. Preheat the oven to 300°F. The brisket will take 3 hours to cook; time the cooking so that it will be ready ½ hour before you want to serve it.

2. Place a large piece of heavy-duty aluminum foil on the counter and sprinkle 1 envelope of onion soup mix over the middle of the foil. Place the brisket fat side up over the soup mix. Sprinkle the other envelope of soup mix over the top of the brisket. Wrap the brisket in the foil like a Christmas package, or use what's called a drugstore wrap around the meat, to make sure that no juices will escape during cooking.

3. Place the brisket in a roasting pan and put in the preheated oven. Cook for 3 hours.

4. When cooked, unwrap the brisket and place it on a cutting board. Slice it thinly crosswise and then twice lengthwise. Make sure you save every drop of the brisket juices from the foil wrap and the cutting board.

5. Place the slices of brisket on a warm platter and drizzle the reserved juices over them just before serving.

Serves 6 to 8 people.

Meat Loaf

This meat loaf is highly seasoned and has a good deal of fat in it. Not a diet morsel.

The mixture is very soft and moist. When browning the loaves, I suggest you use two spatulas to keep them from falling apart as you turn them.

¾ pound ground beef
¼ pound ground pork
1 teaspoon Lawry's seasoned salt
½ teaspoon onion powder
½ teaspoon garlic powder
1 teaspoon Worcestershire sauce
1 8-ounce can tomato sauce
1 teaspoon prepared mustard
1 large egg, lightly beaten
½ cup milk

1 cup soft bread crumbs
Flour for coating
4 tablespoons vegetable oil

1. Mix together the ground beef and ground pork. Add the seasoned salt, onion powder, garlic powder, Worcestershire sauce, tomato sauce, and mustard and mix thoroughly.

2. In a small bowl, combine the lightly beaten egg and milk and then add the bread crumbs. Add this mixture to the meat mixture and combine thoroughly.

3. Divide the meat loaf mixture in half and pat each half into an oval-shaped loaf about 2" thick. Roll each loaf in flour to coat.

4. Heat the vegetable oil in a 9" frying pan over moderate heat. Carefully place the loaves in the pan and brown, turning them carefully. When browned, add enough water to the pan so that it reaches ½" up the sides. Cover the pan, turn down the heat, and let the meat loaves simmer for 45 minutes. You will probably have to keep adding water to the pan as the loaves cook.

VARIATION: You can put the entire meat loaf mixture into a Pyrex loaf pan, cover the loaf with a couple of strips of bacon, and bake it in a preheated 375°F oven for 1 hour. After ½ hour or so, when the bacon starts to get very brown, lightly cover the pan with aluminum foil.

Serves 4 people.

To make soft bread crumbs for this meat loaf, take 2 slices of bread that are several days old, tear them into small pieces, put them in a food processor, and pulse several times.

Lasagna

This recipe serves twenty-four very lucky people, but it can easily be divided in half for twelve fortunate diners.

4 tablespoons olive oil

2 cups chopped onion (about 4 medium onions)

4 cloves garlic, minced

3 pounds ground beef

1 pound ground pork

2 12-ounce cans tomatoes

2 15-ounce cans tomato sauce

5 tablespoons dried parsley flakes or 10 tablespoons chopped fresh

3 tablespoons sugar

2 teaspoons salt

4 teaspoons dried oregano

2 teaspoons dried basil or 1 tablespoon fresh

16 ounces dried lasagna noodles

32 ounces creamy cottage cheese

2 cups grated Parmesan cheese

24 ounces shredded mozzarella cheese

1. Preheat the oven to 400°F.

2. To make the sauce, heat the olive oil in a large frying pan over medium heat. Add the onion and garlic and sauté for a few minutes. Then add the ground beef and ground pork and brown, separating the meat into small pieces as you go. When browned, pour off the fat.

3. To the meat in the frying pan, add the tomatoes, tomato sauce, 3 tablespoons parsley flakes (or 6 tablespoons chopped fresh),

sugar, salt, 2 teaspoons oregano, and the basil, mixing well. Cook over medium heat for about ½ hour, stirring occasionally, until the sauce is thick. Remove from the heat and set aside.

4. Cook the lasagna noodles in a large pot of boiling, salted water until tender but still firm. Drain and pat dry.

5. While the noodles are cooking, combine the cottage cheese, 1 cup of the Parmesan cheese, and the remaining 2 tablespoons parsley flakes (or 4 tablespoons chopped fresh) and 2 teaspoons oregano in a medium bowl. Mix well and set aside.

6. In another medium bowl, combine the remaining 1 cup of Parmesan cheese and the mozzarella cheese. Mix well and set aside.

7. To assemble the lasagna, you will need 2 lasagna pans. In the first pan, line the bottom with a quarter of the cooked noodles. Spread a quarter of the cottage cheese mixture over the noodles. Cover the cottage cheese layer with a quarter of the sauce and then sprinkle a quarter of the Parmesan-mozzarella mixture over the sauce. Repeat each of these layers once, ending with the Parmesan-mozzarella mixture. Then repeat the entire assembly process with the second lasagna pan.

8. Bake the lasagna in the preheated oven for 10 minutes, then reduce the heat to 375°F and bake for 35 minutes more. Let it cool just a little and firm up for a few minutes before cutting and serving it. The lasagna freezes very nicely and can be reheated in a microwave oven.

Serves 24 people.

Grilled Pork Tenderloin

This is a never-fail recipe. Absolutely delicious. Pork tenderloins often come two to a package. I cook one and freeze the other for another time.

¼ cup light brown sugar
¼ cup olive oil
¼ cup soy sauce
¼ cup red wine
4 cloves garlic, crushed (more to taste)
1 pork tenderloin

1. For the marinade, combine the brown sugar, olive oil, soy sauce, red wine, and garlic in a bowl. Place the tenderloin in a large resealable plastic bag and pour the marinade over it. Seal the plastic bag, place it in a large bowl in case it leaks, and leave the tenderloin in the refrigerator for 24 hours to marinate, turning the bag occasionally.

2. Remove the tenderloin carefully from the plastic bag and place it on a plate. Pour the marinade into a saucepan and boil it thoroughly, for 5 to 10 minutes, for basting the tenderloin while it cooks; it's not considered safe to baste with a marinade that has been in contact with raw meat or poultry unless it has been boiled first.

3. To cook the tenderloin, use a gas or charcoal grill. Place the marinated tenderloin over medium flames for 20 to 25 minutes, turning it about every 4 minutes so that all sides get exposed to the flames. Baste the tenderloin all through the cooking period.

Serves 6 people.

Marty's Pork Tenderloin

This dish can be cooked in the morning and reheated before serving, and it will still taste wonderful.

2 pork tenderloins
Salt and ground black pepper to taste
2 tablespoons olive oil
2 cloves garlic, minced
½ tablespoon Worcestershire sauce
½ tablespoon soy sauce
1 teaspoon dried rosemary or 1 tablespoon fresh
1 tablespoon all-purpose flour or cornstarch, dissolved in
    1 cup water
½ cup apricot jam

1. Pat dry the tenderloins and salt and pepper to taste.

2. Heat the olive oil in a large, deep frying pan that has a tight-fitting lid. Sear the tenderloins in the oil, turning to brown all sides. Stir in the garlic, Worcestershire sauce, soy sauce, and rosemary. The pan juices will start to become crusty; scrape them up and stir in the flour or cornstarch and apricot jam.

3. Turn the heat to low and cover the pan. Simmer for about 45 minutes, until the tenderloins are cooked through. You may need to add a little water periodically while they simmer, as the pan juices evaporate. Remove the tenderloins from the pan, slice, and drizzle with any extra pan juices before serving.

Serves 8 people.

Four Ways to Cook Rice

The following recipes are for raw rice—the kind you buy in bulk in plastic bags, not the kind you buy in boxes, such as converted rice and instant rice. To cook raw rice, I strongly advise you to invest in a rice steamer. It's one of the most useful pieces of equipment I own and it's constantly on top of the stove being used, not only for cooking rice and grits but for steaming vegetables, too. In my estimation, it cooks rice and grits better than any other method, and with much less hassle. In Charleston, my local hardware store sells a beauty with a glass cover. The glass is more for looks as far as I'm concerned, but it does give you notice when things are beginning to percolate, because you can see drops of moisture on its inside.

In the following recipes, one cup of raw rice will produce three cups of cooked rice, as the rice swells considerably while cooking. Also, for most occasions, you need about one cup of raw rice for every four or five people.

Steamed Rice

Proportions for steaming rice are as follows: For every cup of raw rice, add 1 cup water and ½ teaspoon salt. The top of the average rice steamer accommodates 2 cups of raw rice. Also, always put plenty of water in the bottom of the steamer so that it doesn't completely boil off.

Put your raw rice in a sieve and rinse under cold running water for a couple of minutes. Let drain. Put into the top of your rice steamer along with the appropriate amount of water and salt and place over the boiling water in the bottom of the steamer. Put the cover on and let the rice steam for 30 minutes or so, until it is tender and the water is absorbed. Fluff the rice with a fork. It's ready to serve at this point, but it can hold in the steamer for a while without any problems. Just fluff again before serving.

To improvise a rice steamer if you don't have the real thing, put the rice, water, and salt in a heatproof bowl. Place the bowl inside a pot deep enough so that the cover will still go on. Also, there must be at least ½" between the sides of the pot and the bowl. Put enough water into the pot so that it reaches two-thirds of the way up the side of the bowl. Bring the water in the pot to a boil, cover, and steam for about 30 minutes, until the rice is tender and the water is absorbed. Fluff with a fork before serving.

I like to serve steamed rice with gravy, but there are a number of ways to prepare it. While the rice is steaming, you can add various cut-up vegetables, such as onion, celery, okra, or zucchini, or meats such as cooked ham or bacon. Or, instead of cooking the rice in water, you can use chicken or beef broth, tomato juice, or tomato soup—let your imagination take wing. Just be sure you have 1 cup of liquid for every cup of raw rice.

Quick Boiled Rice

This method of cooking rice is still used by many good Southern cooks who are such pros at it that they don't even need to measure. Between a practiced eye and hand and a sixth sense, it turns out perfectly every time. I'm not too bad at it myself, though I do measure, and I provide the amounts for you here.

Rinse 1 cup raw rice in a sieve under cold running water and let it drain. Put 1¾ cups water, 2 tablespoons unsalted butter, and ½ teaspoon salt in a medium saucepan. Bring to a boil. Add the rice and stir. Return to a boil and let bubble for 3 or 4 minutes, until the rice has absorbed most of the water. Stir again, turn the heat down to low, cover the saucepan, and let the rice cook for 15 to 20 minutes, until all the water is absorbed. Taste a few grains to see whether the rice is done. If it's still hard in the middle, sprinkle a couple tablespoons of water over the rice, cover the pan, and let it cook a little longer. Fluff with a fork before serving.

I doubt I've sold you on this method of cooking rice, but it's a good one if you're in a hurry. The rice cooks in half the time than with other methods and it tastes just as good and is just as fluffy.

Oven-Cooked Rice

You can cook large amounts of raw rice—6 or 7 cups— this way. When choosing a roasting pan for this method, remember that every cup of raw rice produces 3 cups of cooked, so make sure your pan is large enough for the full cooked amount. Your pan must also have a cover that fits snugly.

Preheat the oven to 350°F. Rinse 6 cups of raw rice under cold running water and drain. Pour into your roasting pan. On top of your stove, bring 12 cups of water and 3 teaspoons of salt to a boil (in this method, it's 2 cups of liquid and ½ teaspoon of salt for every cup of raw rice). Pour the boiling water over the rice in the roasting pan and stir. Put the cover on, place in the preheated oven, and do not look at the rice for 40 or 50 minutes. Do not stir the rice during this time. If you do, your rice will be sticky instead of fluffy; you want every grain to stand on its own. Taste a few grains of rice to see if it is done. If they are still hard in the middle, add a little more water and cook a bit longer. But remember, don't stir.

Aromatic Rice

This recipe is excellent when you don't have gravy. It cooks in a steamer, although you can improvise if you don't have one (see page 174). Put plenty of water in the bottom of the steamer. Rinse 2 cups rice under cold running water and drain. Put in the top of the steamer. Slice a medium onion and chop 2 ribs celery. Melt 4 tablespoons unsalted butter in a skillet over medium heat and sauté the onion and celery until soft and translucent. Do not brown. Pour in 2 cups chicken broth and ¼ cup white wine. Stir to combine and pour over the rice in the steamer. Stir again, cover the steamer, and cook for about 30 minutes, until the rice is tender and the liquid is absorbed. Fluff with a fork before serving.

Hominy Bread

This is a good side dish for beef, chicken, or fish. But of course, anything with a pot of hominy and cheese and eggs in it has some cholesterol.

4 ½ cups water

1 teaspoon salt

1 cup yellow grits

4 tablespoons margarine

2 cups grated garlic cheese or 2 cups grated Cheddar cheese
   plus 1 teaspoon garlic powder

4 large eggs, well beaten

Cornflake crumbs for sprinkling

Margarine for dotting

1. Preheat the oven to 375°F.

2. Bring the 4 ½ cups water to a boil, add the salt, and pour in the grits in a steady stream, stirring all the time. When the mixture begins to thicken, stir in the margarine and cheese. Continue to stir until the margarine and cheese have melted and are well combined. Remove from the heat and stir in the eggs.

3. Pour the mixture into an 8" × 10" casserole dish. Sprinkle with cornflake crumbs, then dot with margarine. Bake in the preheated oven for 30 to 35 minutes. This dish is best when eaten right out of the oven, but it can hold a little while if necessary. It's much more hostess-friendly than a soufflé.

Serves 6 to 8 people.

Stuffed Tomatoes Broiled in a Convection Microwave

A convection microwave is a combination microwave and convection oven. You can use one function at a time or combine the functions. You almost don't need a stove with one. I can't live without mine.

8 small, firm tomatoes (about 3" in diameter)
2 – 3 slices white bread, crusts removed and torn into small pieces
½ cup mayonnaise
½ cup grated Parmesan cheese
Paprika for sprinkling

1. Wash the tomatoes and cut large hollows in the stem ends, removing most of the flesh from inside but leaving enough to keep the tomato cases firm. Do not discard the flesh. Sprinkle the inside

of the tomato cases with salt and pepper and invert them on a rack to drain for about 15 minutes.

2. While the cases are draining, chop the tomato flesh into small pieces and remove the seeds. In a medium bowl, combine the tomato flesh with the bread. Thoroughly mix in the mayonnaise and Parmesan cheese. Stuff each tomato case with some of this filling and sprinkle the top of each with paprika.

3. Broil in a convection microwave for 10 minutes. (You can also broil the tomatoes in a regular oven.) Serve immediately.

Serves 8 people as a side dish.

Green Snap Beans

In some places, snap beans are called string beans. I guess we call them snap beans because you break off the ends where they snap.

1 pound fresh snap beans
1 small onion, diced
2 tablespoons unsalted butter

1. Wash the beans and snap off the ends. Drop them into a pot of boiling, salted water. Do not cover the pot. Bring them back to a boil and cook for 8 to 10 minutes. Taste one every now and then to test if they are done. When they are just tender but still bright green, pour off the water and set them aside.

2. Just before serving, sauté the onion in the butter until translucent and then add the beans to the pan. Continue to cook until the beans are heated through. Serve immediately.

Serves 4 to 6 people.

Microwaved White Onions

This one is so simple, it sounds almost too good to be true, but let me tell you, it's both easy and wonderful. And you can experiment with the recipe to get the taste you like best. Marty uses regular yellow-skinned onions, leaves out the sugar, and cooks them for fourteen minutes in her microwave with a little virgin olive oil in the cut on the top of each onion. We agree that smaller onions—ones about two and a half inches in diameter—are best.

6–8 small white onions
¼ tablespoon unsalted butter
Pinch of sugar
Pinch of salt

1. Peel the onions and cut off the ends. On the top of each onion make a little cut with a sharp knife.

2. Put the onions in a microwaveproof baking dish, along with the butter, sugar, and salt. Stir, cover the dish, and microwave on high for 10 to 12 minutes. Stir again and serve immediately.

Serves 6 people as a side dish.

Peg's Cranberry Salad

*A holiday specialty. We make this salad in a fluted Tupperware mold
with a tube in the middle. The tube comes loose and releases the salad,
which I put on a bed of lettuce and set out on the sideboard for our
Thanksgiving and Christmas buffet dinners. You can also use little
two-ounce individual molds.*

4 cups fresh cranberries
1 cup sugar
1 3-ounce package cherry Jell-O
1 cup orange juice
2 oranges, peeled and slices cut up, or 1 11-ounce can mandarin
    orange slices, drained
2 ribs celery, diced (about 1 cup)
1 8-ounce can crushed pineapple, drained very well
½ teaspoon salt
½ cup chopped pecans (optional)

1. Wash the cranberries and finely chop them in a food processor.
   Sprinkle the sugar over the cranberries and let stand for 15 to 20
   minutes, stirring occasionally.

2. In a large bowl, combine the Jell-O with 1 cup boiling water. Stir
   for a couple of minutes, then add the orange juice. Stir in the
   cranberries, orange slices, celery, pineapple, salt, and, if you like,
   the pecans.

3. Pour the mixture into a 6-cup mold and refrigerate until firm,
   about 4 hours. To serve, unmold over a bed of lettuce.

Serves 10 to 12 people.

Regina's Biscuits

Regina says the secret here is to keep the dough soft. Everybody has their likes and dislikes in regard to biscuits. I want them to rise and be fluffy, but some people prefer them not to rise, but to be very short. The cream of tartar makes them rise, but put in too much and you'll taste it. Don't be afraid to shift things about, but be careful when you do.

2 cups all-purpose flour

4 teaspoons baking powder

⅛ teaspoon cream of tartar

½ teaspoon salt

2 tablespoons sugar

8 tablespoons unsalted butter or ½ cup vegetable shortening,
   chilled and cut into 8 pieces

1 large egg

½ cup milk

1. Preheat the oven to 400°F.

2. In a large bowl, sift together the flour, baking powder, cream of tartar, salt, and sugar. Cut in the butter or shortening. Stir in the egg and milk with a fork. If the dough is not soft, add an additional tablespoon or so of milk.

3. Turn the dough out onto a lightly floured surface and knead 5 or 6 times. With a lightly floured rolling pin, roll out the dough to ½" thickness. Cut out the biscuits using a 2" round biscuit cutter or a sharp knife. (If the knife isn't sharp, the biscuits will not rise properly.) Place the biscuits on an ungreased baking sheet and bake in the preheated oven for 10 to 12 minutes. Serve piping hot.

Makes about 12 biscuits.

Sweet Cream Biscuits

This is the easiest biscuit recipe because there's no butter to cut in. The Southern advice on biscuits: Take two. Butter them liberally. Eat them hot.

1½ cups self-rising flour
1 tablespoon sugar
1 cup heavy cream

1. Preheat the oven to 425°F.

2. In a medium bowl, sift together the flour and sugar. Stir in the cream with a fork.

3. On a lightly floured surface, knead the dough about 6 times. With a lightly floured rolling pin, roll out the dough to ½" thickness. Cut out the biscuits using a 2" round biscuit cutter. If you want to save time, cut out 2" squares with a sharp knife. (If the knife isn't sharp, the biscuits won't rise properly.) Place the biscuits on an ungreased baking sheet and bake in the preheated oven for 10 to 12 minutes. Serve piping hot.

Makes about 12 biscuits.

Wild Fish and Game

O NE OF THE IMPORTANT THINGS TO REMEMBER ABOUT THE GAME YOU ARE cooking is that whatever it is, individual ones are probably different ages and have had different experiences. Some deer are elderly. Some ducks have flown the flyways more often than others. Some have had more to eat than others. Doves, partridges, ducks, and wild turkeys will be more tender if you cook them slowly in moist heat and add fat—oil, butter, or bacon.

Roast Leg of Venison

Ben always thought roast leg of venison was the thing we should have for Christmas dinner at Fox Bank. This recipe comes out wonderfully if you follow the instructions exactly.

1 boned leg of venison (approximately 6 pounds)
1 10-ounce bottle zesty Italian salad dressing
6 tablespoons pickling spices
3 tablespoons whole black peppercorns
4 or 5 bay leaves

1. Put the venison in a large resealable plastic bag.

2. In a small bowl, combine the salad dressing, pickling spices, peppercorns, and bay leaves. Pour into the bag with the venison, seal the bag, and set it in a shallow roasting pan, in case it leaks. Place the pan in the refrigerator and let the venison marinate for no more than 24 hours. Turn the bag 3 or 4 times while the meat is marinating.

3. When ready to cook the roast, preheat the oven to 300°F. Remove the venison from the bag and place it on a rack in a roasting pan. Pour the marinade over the meat and roast in the preheated oven for about 1½ hours, until a meat thermometer registers 155°F. Baste the roast with the marinade in the pan every 20 minutes or so while it is cooking. Carve the roast and serve hot.

Serves 10 to 12 people.

Venison Chili

This recipe comes from Augusta Porcher Kuhn. It's inventive and very good on cold weekends in the country.

2 tablespoons vegetable oil

3 or 4 medium onions, diced

4 cloves garlic, crushed

2 pounds ground venison

2 pounds venison sausage

2 dashes Worcestershire sauce

3 15-ounce cans tomato sauce

3 15-ounce cans diced tomatoes, with their juice

1 6-ounce can tomato paste

1 cup water

2 16-ounce cans kidney beans

1 tablespoon chili powder

1 teaspoon ground cumin

½ teaspoon ground black pepper

2 teaspoons ground oregano

1 teaspoon hot sauce (more to taste)

1. In a large skillet, heat the vegetable oil. Add the onions and cook until soft. Add the garlic, ground venison, and venison sausage. Turn up the heat and cook until the meat is browned, stirring occasionally. Transfer to a large Dutch oven or stewing pot.

2. Stir in the remaining ingredients. Bring the chili to a boil over medium-high heat, stirring constantly. Reduce the heat to low,

cover the pot, and let the chili simmer for the next 1½ to 2 hours, stirring occasionally.

Serves 20 people.

Doves in Foil Packages

I would tell you how to draw and dress the doves, but since I won't do it myself, I'm not the one to tell you anything but this: Make the hunter do it himself.

6 doves, drawn and dressed
Salt and ground black pepper to taste
Paprika to taste
Dried thyme to taste
3 tablespoons unsalted butter
3 teaspoons sherry
3 teaspoons red wine vinegar

1. Preheat the oven to 300°F.

2. Sprinkle each dove with salt, pepper, paprika, and thyme. Put ½ tablespoon butter in the cavity of each dove, followed by ½ teaspoon sherry and ½ teaspoon red wine vinegar.

3. Using heavy-duty aluminum foil, create 3 packets for the doves. Each packet should hold 2 doves. The packets should be securely folded and without any tears, so that none of the juices will escape. Cook in the preheated oven for 2 hours. Unwrap the doves, transfer to a serving plate, and serve immediately.

Serves 2 or 3 people.

Marty's Partridge or Dove Pie

Partridges are plumper than doves, so you need fewer for a pie. Also, you can prepare the birds a day ahead and store them overnight in the refrigerator, filling the pie the next day before baking.

Enough sturdy pastry to line a 3"-deep, 11"-round baking dish and to make a top crust

12 partridges or 24 doves, drawn and dressed

Salt and ground black pepper to taste

½ teaspoon dried rosemary

16 tablespoons unsalted butter

2 tablespoons all-purpose flour

2 14½-ounce cans chicken broth

1. Preheat the oven to 375°F.

2. On a lightly floured surface, with a lightly floured rolling pin, roll out enough of the pastry to line the bottom and sides of the baking dish. Set aside.

3. Rub the birds with salt, pepper, and rosemary. Over medium heat, melt the butter in a deep, heavy pan and brown the birds. Remove them from the pan and keep them warm while you continue with the recipe. Leave the pan over medium heat and add the flour to the butter and juices remaining in it. Whisk out any lumps. Pour in the chicken broth and continue to stir until the gravy has thickened. Add any of the juices that have drained from the reserved birds.

4. Return the birds to the pan and simmer, covered, until they are very tender and the gravy is quite thick. Transfer the birds to the

prepared crust and spoon gravy over them, but do not completely cover the birds with gravy.

5. On a lightly floured surface, with a lightly floured rolling pin, roll out the remaining pastry for the top crust. Cover the pie with it, crimp the edges, and cut 6 steam slits in the top. If you're creative, use any leftover dough to decorate the top—perhaps with shapes of a hunter, gun, and dog! Bake in the preheated oven for about 45 minutes, until the top crust is golden brown.

Serves 8 people handily.

Kershaw's Method for Cooking Wild Duck Breast

Kershaw cleans the wild ducks, then removes the breasts from the bones and discards the rest. He seasons each breast with salt and pepper and then browns them in butter in a skillet (about a tablespoon of unsalted butter for 2 breasts). When the breasts are golden brown all over, he sets each one over a layer of chopped onion on a square of heavy-duty aluminum foil large enough to completely enfold the breast. Then he lays strips of bacon over each breast and wraps each one in the foil like a Christmas package, crimping the seams so the juices won't leak.

The foil packages should be placed in a single layer on a baking sheet. Cook in a preheated 350°F oven for 1 hour. When they are done, remove them from the foil packets, taking care not to let the steam or juices burn your fingers. Set the breasts on a platter and serve with pride. They are especially good with baked rice.

Elijah's Method for Cooking Crabs

If you do it this way, the crabmeat comes out of the shell very easily. Elijah is a perfectly wonderful man who has been the waterer in the garden for years. You need a man to boil crabs, or at least you shouldn't be bothered if a man is available.

But do take your children or grandchildren or any child to catch the crabs. I expect crabbing is one sport that can still be enjoyed along this coast and in a lot of other places. Wild game hunting couldn't offer more excitement for children. Whenever we went crabbing at the beach, Ben cooked the crabs with a lot of screeching and jumping by every child, because some of the crabs always got out of the pot and had to be scooped up and tossed back into the boiling water and, of course, the biggest and most dangerous always ended up behind the refrigerator or under the washing machine. This was Ben's idea of managing the kitchen.

1 gallon water
2 tablespoons salt
4 tablespoons white distilled vinegar
Live crabs

1. In a large pot, bring the water, salt, and vinegar to a jumping, rolling boil. Drop in the live crabs; the pot will hold about 12 crabs at a time. Return to a boil, reduce the heat to medium, and cook the crabs for 15 minutes. No longer than that. The shells will be red.

2. Carefully remove the crabs from the pot and spread out to cool. When cool enough to handle, remove the top shell with one hand, holding the crab down by the claws with the other. You can discard

the shell or keep it for presentation. Turn the crab over and pull off the "dead man" and discard it (the dead man is the triangular breastplate). From the top side, pull off the gills on both sides of the body; these are often called the "dead man's fingers." Remove the intestine (the solid thin white tube) and the gray matter attached to the body. These should be discarded. The soft yellow matter should be removed, too, but it is quite delicious when blended into butter. Rinse the body. You now have only meat and shell. The large claws have particularly good meat in them.

Plan to serve about 2 or 3 crabs per person.

Sweets

———◆———

including Finger Desserts;
Cakes; Pies; Icings, Sauces,
and Fillings; and Other
Confections

Finger Desserts

I KEEP LOOKING FOR A TERM TO REPLACE HOSTESS-FRIENDLY. I'M TOLD THE FRENCH say *"utilitaire,"* but that sounds suspiciously like "utilitarian." So finger desserts will just have to go as very, very hostess-friendly. You serve them with only a napkin, which cuts down on the number of dishes going into the dishwasher. With soup, salad, and a main dish, you've already got the dishwasher full. Every one of the finger desserts here is excellent.

Anne's Thin Ginger Squares

Anne got this one from my great-grandmother's book of recipes.

16 tablespoons unsalted butter, at room temperature

1½ cups sugar

1 cup dark molasses

2 large eggs

1½ cups all-purpose flour, sifted

1 tablespoon ground cinnamon

1 tablespoon ground ginger

½ teaspoon ground cloves

1 teaspoon salt

1. Preheat the oven to 375°F and grease and flour two 8" × 8" × 2" baking pans. Set aside.

2. Cream the butter and sugar in a food processor. Add the molasses and eggs and pulse a few times. Add the flour, cinnamon, ginger, cloves, and salt, pulsing until well combined.

3. Spread the dough in the prepared pans and bake in the preheated oven for 20 minutes. Cut into 2" squares while still hot and remove from the pans to racks for cooling. Store in an airtight container.

Makes 32 squares.

Nan's Thin Cake

Dad had thin cake with a glass of ice tea at the end of every midday dinner. After baking the cake and cutting it into "sticks," just put them in a 195°F oven and let them crisp up—that 195°F is a hostess-friendly temperature for warming just about anything. And the ice tea Nan served with every meal. Sweet tea. I don't know why, but I've never served much ice tea, which is very un-Southern of me. But I do love hot tea. When I turned to all those other sweeteners—the pink envelopes and the blue envelopes—I did find them delicious with tea. My grandson Ben LeClercq came to visit and said they were bad for me. I said I wasn't having bad effects. But he threw them all out when I wasn't looking. So now I'm back to sugar, which isn't as sweet.

2 cups all-purpose flour, sifted

⅛ teaspoon salt

1½ cups sugar

9 tablespoons margarine, chilled and cut into 9 pieces

1 large egg

1½ teaspoons ground cinnamon

1. Preheat the oven to 375°F.

2. Put the flour, salt, and 1 cup of the sugar in the bowl of a food processor and pulse a couple of times. Add the margarine and pulse several times. Add the egg and run the processor steadily for about a minute until the dough forms a ball, stopping once or twice to scrape down the sides of the bowl.

3. Grease and flour a 16" × 10" baking pan. Press the dough evenly into the bottom of the pan. If you have something called a pizza

roller, which looks very much like a small wallpaper roller, it's great for pressing this kind of dough down in the pan.

4. Combine the remaining ½ cup sugar with the cinnamon and sprinkle evenly over the dough in the pan. Bake in the preheated oven for 15 minutes.

5. Immediately cut the cake into 2" × 1" sticks, lift them carefully out of the pan, and place on cooling racks. Reduce the oven temperature to 195°F and place the racks in the oven for 1 hour to crispen the cake sticks. Allow the sticks to cool before storing in an airtight container.

Makes about 60 cake sticks.

Sara Lee's Lemon Bars

She's my friend Sara Lee, not the grocery-store Sara Lee. Her lemon bars are something special. Cut them in small one-inch squares for the fingers or for dessert try two-inch squares with whipped cream on top.

CRUST:
2 cups all-purpose flour
½ cup confectioners' sugar
16 tablespoons unsalted butter, chilled and cut into 16 pieces

FILLING:
4 large eggs
2 cups sugar
⅓ cup fresh lemon juice

¼ cup all-purpose flour
½ teaspoon baking powder
Confectioners' sugar for dusting

1. Preheat the oven to 350°F.

2. For the crust, sift together the flour and confectioners' sugar in a large bowl. Cut in the butter until the mixture clings together. If it doesn't quite hold together, push it together with your hands. Press the dough into a 13" × 9" × 2" baking pan and bake in the preheated oven for 20 minutes.

3. While the crust is baking, beat together the eggs, sugar, and lemon juice in a large bowl.

4. In a small bowl, sift together the flour and baking powder. Stir into the egg-sugar mixture until well combined. Spread over the prebaked crust and bake 25 minutes more, until lightly browned. Remove from the oven and dust with confectioners' sugar. Cool completely in the pan on a rack, then cut into 1" or 2" squares. Store in an airtight container.

Makes about 18 to 36 bars, depending on how small you cut them.

Sara Lee's Almond Squares

Almonds come already slivered, so there's no chopping or slicing to be done. Also, here again the pizza roller is very handy for spreading stiff dough right in the pan.

8 tablespoons unsalted butter, at room temperature
8 tablespoons margarine, at room temperature
1 cup sugar
1 large egg, separated
2 cups all-purpose flour, sifted
Dash of salt
2 teaspoons vanilla or almond extract
1 cup slivered almonds

1. Preheat the oven to 275°F.

2. With an electric mixer, cream the butter, margarine, and sugar in a large bowl. Beat in the egg yolk, flour, salt, and vanilla or almond extract.

3. Press the dough evenly into a 15" × 10" × 1" baking pan.

4. Gently beat the egg white until it is slightly foamy. With a pastry brush, spread it over the top of the dough. Immediately sprinkle the almonds over the top. Bake in the preheated oven for 45 minutes. Remove from the oven and wait 10 minutes before cutting into 3 ½" squares. Let cool completely and store in an airtight container.

Makes 15 squares.

Peg's Meringues

Meringues should not be made on a rainy day. They keep well for up to a week in an airtight container, so they can be made well ahead of time and used as a base for ice cream and sauce or other desserts.

4 egg whites
Pinch of salt
1 teaspoon white distilled vinegar
1 cup sugar
1 teaspoon almond extract

1. Line a couple of large baking sheets with parchment paper. Set aside.

2. Beat the egg whites with an electric mixer at medium speed until frothy. Add the salt and vinegar. Add 1 tablespoon of the sugar at a time, beating well after each addition. This is the secret to making perfect meringues. It gives the sugar a chance to dissolve, which keeps the meringues from being grainy.

3. Turn the mixer up to high speed, add the almond extract, and continue to beat until the egg whites form stiff peaks and are shiny but not dry.

4. Drop from a tablespoon onto the prepared baking sheets, making 2" circles. Place in a cold oven, turn the oven temperature to 250°F, and bake for 1 hour. Turn off the oven but leave the meringues inside for 2 hours more.

Makes about 48 meringues.

Oatmeal Lace Cookies

This recipe yields about two hundred very small cookies. Although it is time-consuming to make so many, they keep well in a tin or can be frozen, and they make an unusually nice present.

2 cups quick-cooking oats
2 cups sugar
2 large eggs, well beaten
16 tablespoons unsalted butter, melted
6 tablespoons all-purpose flour
½ teaspoon salt
½ teaspoon baking powder
1 teaspoon vanilla extract

1. Preheat the oven to 350°F and line 3 baking sheets with aluminum foil or parchment paper. Do not grease the foil or paper. Set aside.

2. In a large bowl, combine the oats, sugar, eggs, and butter. Mix well.

3. In a small bowl, sift together the flour, salt, and baking powder. Stir into the oats until well combined. Stir in the vanilla extract.

4. Drop by the ½ teaspoonful onto the prepared baking sheets, being careful to keep 2 inches between the cookies. Bake in the preheated oven for 10 minutes. Set the baking sheets on racks to cool, then carefully peel the foil or parchment paper from the cookies.

5. Put new foil or parchment paper on the baking sheets and repeat step #4 until all the cookie dough is used up. It will take about 1½ hours to bake all the cookies.

Makes about 200 small cookies.

Lizetta's Brownies

Lizetta's mother gave the recipe to her and she gave it to me. I don't believe these brownies can be beat. The recipe is also in Charleston's Junior League cookbook.

8 tablespoons unsalted butter or margarine

3 ounces unsweetened chocolate

2 cups sugar

2 large eggs

1 teaspoon vanilla extract

1 cup all-purpose flour

¼ teaspoon salt

1 cup chopped pecans

1. Preheat the oven to 350°F and grease an 11" × 7" baking pan. Set aside.

2. In the top of a double boiler over hot water, melt the butter or margarine and chocolate, stirring regularly. Remove from the heat and stir in the sugar, eggs, and vanilla extract. Sift in the flour and salt and stir until well combined. Fold in the pecans.

3. Pour the batter into the prepared pan and bake in the preheated oven until the top is crusty and firm but the inside is still soft, about 20 to 25 minutes. Remove from the oven and let cool for 3 to 5 minutes. Cut into 1⅛" squares but cool completely before removing from the pan.

Makes about 30 brownies.

Brown Sugar Brownies

One of my granddaughters, I can't remember which, prefers these to the chocolate ones.

8 tablespoons unsalted butter, melted
2 cups light brown sugar
2 large eggs
2 teaspoons vanilla extract
1½ cups all-purpose flour
2 teaspoons baking powder
½ teaspoon salt
½ cup chopped pecans or walnuts

1. Preheat the oven to 350°F and grease a 9" × 13" baking pan.
   Set aside.

2. In a large bowl, thoroughly combine the butter, brown sugar, eggs,
   and vanilla extract.

3. In a medium bowl, sift together the flour, baking powder, and salt.
   Thoroughly combine with the butter-sugar mixture. Fold in the
   nuts.

4. Spread the mixture in the prepared pan and bake in the preheated
   oven for 20 to 25 minutes. Cut into 2½" squares when cool.
   Store in an airtight container.

Makes 20 brownies.

Dancing School Fudge

This is the fudge I used to bribe the children at our dancing school to learn the steps we were trying to teach them. There were a lot of children to bribe and the fact this fudge is made in less than fifteen minutes in a microwave made the bribery less of a burden than making regulation fudge for such a crowd would have been. Anyway, I suspect I could write a whole book on this one, but I won't — I've already given it a chapter. What I will say is this: No two microwave ovens seem to put out exactly the same heat. You may need to add a little time to the second cooking if the fudge doesn't harden properly. Experiment a bit and note the results for future reference.

8 tablespoons margarine, at room temperature and cut into
    16 pieces (do *not* use butter)
1½ cups sugar
Pinch of salt
1 5-ounce can evaporated milk
1 cup miniature marshmallows
1 6-ounce package semi-sweet chocolate chips
1 teaspoon vanilla extract

1. Coat an 8" × 8" (or 7" × 10") baking pan with vegetable oil cooking spray. Set aside.

2. Thoroughly combine all the ingredients except the vanilla extract in an 8-cup Pyrex measuring pitcher (a handle is essential). Cover the pitcher with a piece of wax paper and microwave on high for 6 minutes (add 30 seconds if you believe your microwave isn't all that powerful).

3. Remove the pitcher and beat vigorously with a wire whisk for at least 30 seconds; the longer you beat, the creamier the fudge will

be. Re-cover the pitcher and microwave on high for 5 ½ minutes (or up to 7 minutes, depending on the heat your oven puts out). Again remove the pitcher and whisk vigorously for at least 30 seconds. Stir in the vanilla extract.

4. Spread the fudge evenly in the prepared pan. When it has set but is still warm, cut into 1" squares. To avoid ragged edges, spray your knife often with vegetable oil cooking spray. Remove from the pan when completely cool. Stored in an airtight container, the fudge will keep for at least a week.

Makes 64 squares.

White Chocolate Nuggets

This is as good a finger dessert as I know of.

½ pound white chocolate, chopped
½ cup shelled dry-roasted peanuts
½ cup thin pretzel sticks, broken into pieces
½ cup Golden Grahams cereal

1. Melt the chocolate in the top of a double boiler over boiling water. You must stir constantly or the chocolate will scorch. Remove from the heat. Stir in the peanuts, pretzel pieces, and cereal. You may not need the full amounts or you may need a little more, depending on how much melted chocolate you have.

2. Cover several baking sheets with wax paper and coat the paper with vegetable oil cooking spray. Drop the chocolate mixture by the teaspoonful onto the paper. When set, store in an airtight container.

Makes 3 to 4 dozen nuggets.

Cakes

YES, THERE ARE INDIVIDUALS STILL BAKING WONDERFUL CAKES FOR SALE, and some bakeries do quite well. Church sales, bazaars, are the best place to look, but you have to get there early because they go quickly. Still you know, people today just don't bake that way anymore. In the olden days, the Ladies Exchange did fill a grievous need, and not just by providing us with delicious homemade cakes. Women hadn't actually been trained to make a living and yet they needed spending money. Many women made things and sent them to the Ladies Exchange. They used to make pincushions, bureau covers, baby bonnets (Charleston was famous for those baby bonnets), exquisite lace, bassinets, and peach "leather," as well as all sorts of other sweets. But there's no place like that today that would take things sent in from the country on consignment. Cross-stitch and all such, women love that sort of thing and they're good at it because they have small muscles. Is that sexist talk? Too bad. I know about those small muscles. If you try to teach both a boy and a girl to do the lindy, she'll learn it three times as fast, because she can handle her feet. It takes a boy a long time to get his feet moving. Anyway, the Ladies Exchange here closed around 1940 or earlier.

Sour Cream Pound Cake

This is an elegant pound cake. When you have a houseful of people, keep one on the counter so that anybody needing a snack can just cut off a piece. But don't overcook it. You must pay attention. Rosie won't eat an overdone pound cake.

8 tablespoons unsalted butter, at room temperature
½ cup vegetable shortening, at room temperature
3 cups sugar
6 large eggs, separated
3 cups cake flour
¼ teaspoon baking powder
¼ teaspoon baking soda
¼ teaspoon salt
1 cup sour cream

1. Preheat the oven to 325°F and grease and flour a 10" × 4" tube pan. Set aside.

2. With an electric mixer, cream the butter and shortening in a large bowl. Gradually add the sugar, beating well after each addition. Add the egg yolks one at a time, beating well after each addition.

3. In a medium bowl, sift together the flour, baking powder, baking soda, and salt. Gradually add to the butter-egg mixture, alternating with the sour cream and ending with the flour mixture.

4. In a large bowl, beat the egg whites until they form stiff peaks but are not dry. Fold a quarter of them into the cake batter, then fold the batter into the remaining egg whites.

5. Pour the batter into the prepared pan and bake in the preheated oven for 1½ hours or until a toothpick inserted in the center comes out clean. Cool in the pan for 10 minutes, then remove from the pan and cool completely.

Serves 12 people.

Eggless Applesauce Cake

I like this cake better than regular fruitcake — it's not so rich and concentrated. The cake takes a long time to cool, so make it in the morning.

16 tablespoons margarine, at room temperature
2 cups sugar
4 cups applesauce
3 cups all-purpose flour
1 teaspoon salt
1 teaspoon baking soda
1 teaspoon ground cinnamon
1 teaspoon ground allspice
1 pound raisins
2 cups chopped candied fruit (often available as "fruitcake mix" at Christmastime)
3 cups whole or chopped pecans

1. Preheat the oven to 325°F. Line an angel food cake pan with wax paper and grease the paper with vegetable shortening. Set aside.

2. With an electric mixer, cream the margarine and sugar in a large bowl. Beat in the applesauce.

3. In a medium bowl, sift together the flour, salt, baking soda, cinnamon, and allspice. Add to the applesauce mixture and beat until well combined. Fold in the raisins, candied fruit, and pecans.

4. Pour the batter into the prepared pan and bake in the preheated oven for 1¾ hours or until a toothpick inserted in the center comes out clean. (Sometimes it takes closer to 2 hours.) Completely cool on a rack before removing from the pan. After removing from the pan, carefully peel away the wax paper if it's sticking to the cake.

Serves at least 20 people.

Ben LeClercq's Favorite Rum Cake

I made this for him one day and he took a tremendous fancy to it. I make it for him often.

1 cup chopped pecans
4 large eggs
1 package yellow cake mix
1 3-ounce package instant vanilla pudding
½ cup water
½ cup vegetable oil
½ cup light rum

GLAZE:
8 tablespoons unsalted butter
1 cup sugar
¼ cup water
¼ cup light rum

1. Preheat the oven to 325°F and grease and flour a Bundt cake pan. Spread the pecans over the bottom of the pan and set aside.

2. With an electric mixer, beat the eggs until they are a light lemon color. Add the cake mix, pudding mix, water, vegetable oil, and rum. Beat until thoroughly combined. Pour into the prepared pan and bake in the middle of the preheated oven for 55 to 60 minutes, until a toothpick inserted in the cake comes out clean. Remove the cake from the oven and let it cool for 5 minutes before removing it from the pan.

3. Toward the end of the cake's baking, make the glaze. In a medium saucepan, bring the butter, sugar, water, and rum to a boil. Reduce the heat to low and let the mixture continue to simmer for 3 minutes. Remove from the heat. While the cake is still warm, poke small holes in the top with a carving fork and pour the hot glaze over the cake. Let the cake sit for an hour before serving to absorb the glaze.

VARIATION: This may be gilding the lily, but it's a treat: Glaze the cake a second time! An hour after applying the first glaze, melt 4 tablespoons unsalted butter in a medium saucepan. Stir in 1 cup light brown sugar, 1 tablespoon cornstarch, ½ cup water, and ½ cup light rum. Bring this to a boil and stir until it has thickened. Pour the hot glaze over the cake and let it sit for another hour before serving.

Serves 8 to 10 people.

Chocolate Waldorf Cake

If you're an Einstein, you'll manage this recipe. Get your IQ tested before you start. (I know this will tempt some of you who want to prove something; the rest of us have been given fair warning.)

I figured that giving this cake as a present would make me solid with anybody. My friend Louisa, the author of the recipe, willingly gave it to me, but I've tried three times and still don't have it right.

1 cup sugar
2 cups all-purpose flour
4 tablespoons unsweetened cocoa
2 teaspoons baking soda
Pinch of salt
1 cup cold water
1 teaspoon vanilla extract
1 cup mayonnaise (not a diet brand)
2 heaping tablespoons blackberry jam

1. Preheat the oven to 350°F and grease and flour two 9" cake pans. Set aside.

2. Sift together the sugar, flour, cocoa, baking soda, and salt in a large bowl. Sift again. Add the water, vanilla extract, mayonnaise, and blackberry jam and stir until well blended.

3. Divide the batter between the 2 prepared cake pans and bake in the preheated oven for 25 to 30 minutes, until a toothpick inserted in the center comes out clean. Cool the cake layers in the pan on a rack for 5 minutes. Remove the layers from the pans and continue cooling on racks. When completely cool, carefully remove one

layer to a cake plate. Spread Smooth Fudge Frosting (see page 224) over the top of that layer and carefully place the other layer on top of it. Frost the top of the second layer and the sides of the cake.

Serves 8 to 10 people.

Aunt Alicia's Lady Baltimore Cake

This is the original recipe for the cake Owen Wister wrote of in his novel Lady Baltimore. *A delicious cake. The secret is that it is a firm layer cake—that and the soft icing, which isn't really an icing at all, but a sauce. Most layer cakes would go to pieces if you poured on such a thin sauce.*

This truly is a secret recipe I'm giving you. My friend Mona somehow got hold of the recipe but never shared it. I went to her and said, "If I promise as long as I live never to give this recipe away, would you let me have it?" I stuck by that promise and never told a soul for twenty-five years. But last year I called the originator's granddaughter and told her I was making a recipe book for my children and I hoped to verify the recipe and include it in the cookbook. She agreed, Mona's recipe and the original matched, and so here you are.

1 cup raisins
1 cup sherry
2 cups cake flour
¼ teaspoon salt
2 teaspoons baking powder
8 tablespoons unsalted butter, at room temperature
1¼ cups sugar
¾ cup milk

1 teaspoon almond extract

3 egg whites, at room temperature

SOFT ICING:

1 cup sugar

½ cup water

1 teaspoon vanilla extract

1 teaspoon almond extract

HARD ICING:

2 cups sugar

½ cup water

2 egg whites, beaten until frothy

½ teaspoon cream of tartar

Juice of 1 lemon

1 teaspoon almond extract

1 cup chopped black walnuts

1. Soak the raisins in the sherry for several hours.

2. Preheat the oven to 375°F and grease and flour two 8" cake pans. Set aside.

3. Sift together the flour, salt, and baking powder several times. Set aside.

4. Cream the butter and sugar in a large bowl. Alternately add the flour and milk in 3 parts, beating well after each addition. Stir in the almond extract.

5. In a large bowl, beat the egg whites until they are stiff but not dry. Fold a quarter of them into the batter, then fold the batter into the remaining egg whites. Divide the batter between the 2 prepared

cake pans and bake in the preheated oven for 20 to 25 minutes, until a toothpick inserted in the center comes out clean.

6. While the cake is baking, prepare the soft icing. Blend the sugar and water in a small saucepan. Heat just long enough to dissolve the sugar. Remove from the heat and add the vanilla and almond extracts. When the cake layers have cooled for 5 minutes in the pan on a rack, remove them from the pans and, while still hot, spoon the icing over them.

7. To make the hard icing, boil the sugar and water in a medium saucepan until a very thin, long thread drops from a spoon. If you're using a candy thermometer, which I advise you to do, it should register between 238°F and 240°F. Pour the boiling liquid in a thin stream over the egg whites, beating continuously with an electric mixer. Add the cream of tartar, lemon juice, and almond extract. Continue beating for about 4 minutes, until soft peaks form.

8. Spread the hard icing over the top of each of the cooled layers. Drain the raisins and sprinkle them over the top of each layer, then sprinkle the walnuts over the top of each layer. Carefully transfer one layer to a cake plate and then place the second layer on top of it. Spread icing on the sides of the cake. Allow the icing to harden before serving.

Serves 12 people.

Mary's Lemon Fluff Cake

This cake is a favorite with my family, especially at Christmas, but it's not the sort of thing you can set on the sideboard and let people nibble on. Eat this one immediately and all at once.

1 angel food cake, homemade or store-bought
6 large eggs, separated
Juice of 3 lemons
1 tablespoon lemon zest
1½ cups sugar
1 envelope Knox unflavored gelatin, dissolved in ¼ cup water
1 cup heavy cream, whipped, or 1 pint nondairy whipped topping
Lemon and orange slices for decoration

1. Tear the angel food cake into small pieces and set aside in a large bowl.

2. With an electric mixer, blend the egg yolks, lemon juice, lemon zest, and ¾ cup of the sugar. Remove to the top of a double boiler over hot water and stir until the lemon mixture is thick enough to coat a wooden spoon, about 10 minutes. Remove from the heat and stir in the gelatin.

3. In a large bowl, beat the egg whites, adding 1 tablespoon at a time of the remaining ¾ cup sugar. Continue beating until the egg whites form soft peaks. Fold a third of the egg whites into the cooled lemon mixture, then fold the lemon mixture into the remaining egg whites. Pour this mixture over the angel food cake and combine well.

4. Pour the batter into a lightly greased angel food cake pan and press down gently with the back of a wooden spoon. Refrigerate for at least 2 hours.

5. When ready to serve, turn the cake out onto a cake plate, frost the entire cake with the whipped cream or nondairy whipped topping, and decorate with the lemon and orange slices.

Serves 8 to 10 people.

Pies

BEN LECLERCQ SAYS THAT HIS BROTHER KERSHAW CAN TAKE MORE LIBERTIES WITH a pie recipe than most people can and still have it come out exactly right. Kershaw just gets this quizzical look on his face like he's going to pull a rabbit out of his hat and he does it every time. All the rest of us are irritated because we have to stick to a quarter teaspoon of this and whip that just so many times. But there's Kershaw slinging every kind of ingredient around the kitchen and he gets perfection. And he loves it and lets you taste the outcome with a devilish grin on his face.

Pâte Brisée

This pastry is ideal for pies and tarts both sweet and savory, and it can be made easily in a food processor.

1⅓ cups all-purpose flour, sifted
½ teaspoon salt
1 tablespoon sugar (for sweet pies and tarts only)
8 tablespoons unsalted butter, chilled and cut into 8 pieces
¼ cup ice water

1. In the bowl of a food processor, combine the flour and salt (and sugar if used) with a few quick pulses.

2. Add the butter and process until the mixture is the consistency of coarse meal, about 5 to 10 seconds.

3. With the processor running, add the ice water in a steady stream through the feed tube. Process for about 15 seconds. If a ball of dough has not formed above the blade, remove the dough and gently form it into one. The dough may be used immediately or chilled for use in the next several days.

4. If the dough has been refrigerated, let it sit at room temperature for 10 minutes before rolling it out. Place the dough on a lightly floured surface and, with a lightly floured rolling pin, roll it out to form an 11" circle about ⅛" thick. Gently transfer the dough to a 9" pie pan and press it into place. Proceed with your pie or tart recipe according to the instructions.

Makes a single 9" crust.

Kershaw's Chocolate Pie

Here it is—Kershaw's chocolate pie, or at least an approximation thereof. You must add the enthusiasm and Lord knows what else.

You can use a store-bought graham cracker crust for this pie, but I give instructions for a good, easy one in Fred's Lemon Pie (see page 219).

1 9" graham cracker crust
1 6-ounce package semi-sweet chocolate chips
1⅓ cups light corn syrup
3 large eggs, well beaten
⅓ cup sugar
3 tablespoons unsalted butter, melted
½ teaspoon salt

1. Preheat the oven to 325°F.

2. Sprinkle the chocolate chips over the bottom of the pie crust. Set aside.

3. In a large bowl, thoroughly combine the corn syrup, eggs, sugar, butter, and salt. Pour into the pie crust and bake in the preheated oven for 30 to 45 minutes, until the filling is thickened and semi-firm. Serve at room temperature.

Serves 6 to 8 people.

Fred's Lemon Pie

I have often told the story of my son-in-law Fred LeClercq going out in a hurricane to get the ingredients for a lemon pie. Well, this is the pie. Fred's father brought the recipe home from the 1939 world's fair. Then Fred began to use it and now his son Kershaw does, too.

CRUST:

8 tablespoons unsalted butter or margarine
1½ cups graham cracker crumbs (about 18 graham crackers)
⅓–½ cup sugar, to taste

FILLING:

4 egg yolks
½ cup fresh lemon juice
2 14-ounce cans sweetened condensed milk

MERINGUE TOPPING:

4 egg whites
½ teaspoon cream of tartar
¾ cup sugar

1. Preheat the oven to 350°F.

2. To make the crust, melt the butter or margarine in a medium saucepan, then quickly stir in the graham cracker crumbs and sugar. Remove from the heat and press into the bottom and sides of a 9" pie plate. Set aside.

3. To make the filling, thoroughly blend the egg yolks, lemon juice, and condensed milk. Pour into the prepared crust and bake in the preheated oven for 7 or 8 minutes. Remove from the oven and allow to cool.

4. When the pie has cooled, prepare the meringue topping. With an electric mixer, beat the egg whites and cream of tartar until well combined. Add 1 tablespoon of the sugar at a time, beating well after each addition. Continue beating until the egg whites form soft peaks. Spread the meringue over the top of the pie and place under the broiler for about a minute to brown, watching carefully to prevent burning. If you prefer, you can brown the meringue in a preheated 425°F oven for 4 or 5 minutes. I like the texture of the meringue better when it has been broiled. Allow to cool before serving.

Serves 6 to 8 people.

Gertie's Lemon Chiffon Pie

Gertie was my mother's cook later on and this pie was a favorite at Flat Rock.

CRUST:

4 tablespoons unsalted butter

3 tablespoons sugar

½ cup graham cracker crumbs (about 6 graham crackers)

18 – 20 vanilla wafers

FILLING:

½ cup fresh lemon juice

1½ envelopes Knox unflavored gelatin, dissolved in ¼ cup water

4 large eggs, separated

1¼ cups sugar

Pinch of salt

1 cup heavy cream

1. In a small saucepan, melt the butter. Quickly stir in the sugar and graham cracker crumbs. Press into the bottom of a 9" pie plate. Line the sides of the plate with vanilla wafers. Set aside.

2. Gently heat the lemon juice and combine with the gelatin. Set aside.

3. In a medium bowl, thoroughly blend the egg yolks, ¾ cup of the sugar, and the salt. Pour this mixture into the top of a double boiler and stir in the gelatin. Over boiling water, stir the mixture until it is smooth and thick enough to coat a wooden spoon. Remove from the heat.

4. In a large bowl, beat the egg whites, adding ¼ cup sugar 1 tablespoon at a time, until they form soft peaks. Fold the lemon—egg yolk mixture into the egg whites until well combined. Pour into the prepared pie crust and refrigerate until firm, about 3 hours.

5. Whip the heavy cream, adding the remaining ¼ cup sugar 1 tablespoon at a time, until it forms soft peaks. Spread decoratively over the top of the chilled pie and serve immediately.

Serves 6 to 8 people.

Icings, Sauces, and Fillings

PRACTICE, PRACTICE, PRACTICE, AND THEN THE WEATHER HAS TO BE JUST RIGHT FOR that icing to turn out. People don't think the weather matters, but you need a sunshiny day to make good icing—a startlingly sunshiny day. A rainy day won't do. The same is true for divinity fudge. Maybe it's the barometric pressure. I don't know what it is, but I do know when to make my icings and fudge.

Belvidere Soft Chocolate Icing

This recipe is ancient. I suspect my Virginia grandmother brought it with her from that state. I've never come across it anywhere. Belvidere was the plantation where my mother was raised.

This chocolate icing is like custard in that they both depend on a sixth sense. You have to take the icing off the heat at just the right time and you have to judge that time by how it looks. It can't be too thin or too thick. To be a good judge you have to make the icing two or three times. If you get it exactly right, the icing never hardens on the cake, but it doesn't run off it either. One thing I've learned is that if you grease your pot two inches from the top with butter or lard, whatever's in that pot won't boil over—it won't go any higher than the grease ring.

4 ounces unsweetened chocolate

1 cup hot water

1½ cups sugar

1 cup milk

3 tablespoons unsalted butter

1 teaspoon vanilla extract

1. Grease the top 2 inches of the inside of the saucepan you'll be using: This will keep the chocolate mixture from boiling over. Put the chocolate and hot water into this saucepan and melt the chocolate over a low heat, stirring constantly. Stir in the sugar and milk.

2. Turn up the heat to medium and bring to a very slow boil. Cook for about 30 minutes, stirring every 5 minutes or so. You must watch this icing carefully to see that it doesn't boil over or scorch.

3. Remove from the heat and stir in the butter until it melts and then the vanilla extract. Spread over your cake right away.

Makes enough to ice a 9" or 10" 2-layer cake.

Smooth Fudge Frosting

This is the right frosting to top off the Chocolate Waldorf Cake (see page 210). Actually, it's this frosting, not the cake itself, that requires a high IQ. The recipe comes from the Charleston Junior League's cookbook, the first one. Unbelievable when it comes out right, but you will definitely need a heavy-bottomed saucepan to succeed.

3 tablespoons vegetable shortening
3 tablespoons margarine
1½ tablespoons light corn syrup
3 ounces unsweetened chocolate, cut into small pieces
½ cup plus 2 tablespoons milk
2¼ cups sugar
¼ teaspoon salt
1½ teaspoons vanilla extract

1. In a heavy-bottomed saucepan, combine all the ingredients except the vanilla extract. Place over the lowest heat possible and gradually bring to a boil, being sure to watch carefully and stir regularly. Let boil for 1 minute only. Remove from the heat and let cool.

2. Add the vanilla extract and beat until smooth, preferably with an electric mixer. Spread over the cake as directed in the recipe.

Makes enough to frost a 9" 2-layer cake.

White Mountain Icing

This is another wonderful icing from my childhood. I add some lemon juice to give it a little zip.

❧

1½ cups sugar
½ teaspoon cream of tartar
½ cup water
2 egg whites, at room temperature
1 teaspoon vanilla or almond extract (I prefer almond)
Juice and zest of 1 lemon
¼ cup boiling water

1. Sift together the sugar and cream of tartar into a small saucepan. Stir in the ½ cup water. Bring to a boil over high heat, stirring until the sugar is dissolved. Cover the saucepan and continue to boil for 2 minutes more. Uncover the saucepan and continue to boil the mixture for about 5 minutes, until it reaches the soft-ball stage, when a small quantity dropped into chilled water forms a ball that does not disintegrate when picked up with your fingers (about 235°F on a candy thermometer).

2. While the syrup is getting to the soft-ball stage, beat the egg whites with an electric mixer until they form soft peaks. When the syrup reaches the soft-ball stage, pour it into the egg whites in a steady stream, beating constantly at high speed until the mixture has cooled and forms stiff, glossy peaks. Beat in the vanilla or almond extract, the lemon juice and zest, and the boiling water. Continue to beat the icing until it has cooled almost to room temperature. Frost your cake as your recipe instructs.

Makes enough to ice one 9" 2- or 3-layer cake or one 10" tube cake.

Bettina's Icing

This is the icing I superstitiously make for all second weddings. It is excellent on fruitcake and pound cake. When the icing has hardened on the cake, I decorate it with sugar ivy leaves and vines (see page 227). An electric mixer is a must for this icing.

2 egg whites
2 cups sugar
1 cup water
8 regular marshmallows
3 tablespoons fresh lemon juice

1. Beat the egg whites with an electric mixer until they are stiff but not dry. Set aside.

2. In a medium saucepan, boil the sugar and water until the mixture reaches the stage where a thin thread flies away from your spoon. Pour half this syrup slowly into the egg whites, beating continuously. Leave the other half to simmer on the stove.

3. Add the marshmallows one at a time to the hot egg white mixture, beating continuously. Beat in the lemon juice. Add the remaining syrup slowly while beating and continue to beat until the icing reaches a consistency that is spreadable.

Makes enough to ice a 10" pound cake.

Sugar Ivy Leaves

These are the ivy leaves that go with Bettina's Icing (see page 226) on all second-wedding cakes. Sometimes I make camellia leaves as well to decorate a cake.

✳

1 pound confectioners' sugar
½ teaspoon cream of tartar
3 egg whites, unbeaten
About 20 freshly cut ivy leaves, untorn and flat

1. Combine the sugar, cream of tartar, and egg whites in a large bowl. With an electric mixer, beat until the mixture is thick enough to spread, but not stiff.

2. With a pastry brush, spread the sugar mixture over the side of each ivy leaf that shows the veins best. Lay each one carefully on wax paper, sugar side up, and leave in a cool, dry place for at least 24 hours, but 72 is even better.

3. Very carefully pull the real ivy leaves away from the sugar leaves. They store for up to a week in an airtight plastic container. When decorating with them, you can use a small amount of the same sugar mixture in a pastry bag to make vines for the leaves. A little of the sugar mixture will also help secure the leaves to the cake.

Makes enough leaves to decorate a 10" pound cake.

Mary's Lemon Sauce

This lemon sauce is a bit different and can be used in many ways. It's wonderful over ice cream and, when thickened some more, it makes a fine pie filling.

8 tablespoons unsalted butter, at room temperature
⅔–1 cup sugar (1 cup makes the sauce too sweet for my taste)
1 large egg, well beaten
Juice of 2 lemons
Zest of 1 lemon
½ teaspoon ground nutmeg
3 tablespoons boiling water

1. Cream the butter and sugar in a large bowl. Add the egg, lemon juice, lemon zest, and nutmeg. Mix well.

2. Transfer the mixture to the top of a double boiler over hot water. Add the 3 tablespoons boiling water and stir constantly with a wooden spoon until the lemon sauce has thickened. Remove from the heat and use as desired.

Makes 1½ cups.

Raspberry Sauce

Use this sauce over vanilla ice cream, poached pears, or baked custard. Raspberries are very "stylish." I generally use the lemon sauce (see above), but in North Carolina in the summer you can get good fresh raspberries. Still expensive, though. I call them a North Carolina treat.

2 10-ounce packages frozen raspberries (use fresh if in season)
¼ cup superfine sugar
2−3 tablespoons orange-flavored liqueur

1. Let the raspberries thaw and then force them through a fine sieve.

2. In a food processor, thoroughly blend the raspberries with the sugar and liqueur. Chill in the refrigerator for a couple of hours before serving.

Makes about 1½ cups.

Hot Chocolate Sauce for Vanilla Ice Cream

Ice cream was such a treat when I was a child. We had no refrigeration or ice to speak of, so churning ice cream was quite a production. It snowed once in my younger days and I remember Cousin Deas Porcher scooping up some snow and pouring Eagle Brand condensed milk over it. Very good. I must have been four years old and all subsequent ice cream treats have had to compete with that one. This hot chocolate sauce comes close.

12 ounces semi-sweet chocolate
½ cup hot strong coffee or room-temperature orange-flavored liqueur
1 14-ounce can sweetened condensed milk
1 7-ounce jar marshmallow fluff
1 teaspoon vanilla extract

1. Put the chocolate and coffee or liqueur in the top of a double boiler over boiling water. Stir until the chocolate melts. Stir in the condensed milk and marshmallow fluff until well blended. Stir in the vanilla extract. Remove from the heat and serve immediately.

2. If you do not want to use the sauce immediately or if you have some left over, store it in an airtight container in the refrigerator. Reheat in a double boiler before serving, stirring regularly.

Makes about 4 cups.

Catherine's Lemon Icing and Meringue Topping for a Cake

I always asked Catherine for this for my birthday. It's especially good on a yellow layer cake.

LEMON ICING:
Juice of 2 ½ lemons
1 tablespoon lemon zest
1 ½ cups sugar
4 egg yolks
3 tablespoons all-purpose flour
4 tablespoons unsalted butter
1 ½ cups boiling water

MERINGUE TOPPING:
4 egg whites
1 cup sugar
½ teaspoon cream of tartar

1. In the top of a double boiler, combine the lemon juice, lemon zest, sugar, egg yolks, and flour. Place over hot water and add the butter and boiling water, stirring until the mixture thickens. Remove from the heat and pour over your cake. The icing is much like a custard, but if it's thick enough it will stay on the cake.

2. To make the meringue topping, beat the egg whites, adding 1 tablespoon of the sugar at a time. Add the cream of tartar while beating. Beat the egg whites until they form stiff peaks and are shiny but not dry. Drop dollops of the meringue over the top of the cake. Place the cake under the broiler for 1 minute to brown the meringue, but watch carefully to prevent burning. You can also bake the cake for 4 or 5 minutes in a preheated 425°F oven, but the texture of the broiled meringue is nicer, even if the technique is a trifle riskier.

Makes enough for a 9" 2-layer cake.

Fruit Filling for Tarts

I like to use this filling for Bama tartlet shells. I buy them in the freezer section of the supermarket; they're about two and a half inches across. The filling is quick and it can be made three or four days ahead of time. But don't buy your tart shells too far in advance. If they sit in the freezer for too long, they get a bit hard and tough.

1 11-ounce can mandarin orange slices, drained
1 8-ounce can crushed pineapple, drained (reserve the juice)
¼ cup sugar
2 tablespoons cornstarch
⅛ teaspoon salt
½ cup orange juice
1 tablespoon fresh lemon juice
½ teaspoon almond extract

1. In a medium bowl, combine the mandarin orange slices and crushed pineapple. Set aside.

2. In a medium saucepan, combine the sugar, cornstarch, salt, orange juice, lemon juice, almond extract, and reserved pineapple juice. Over a medium heat, stir with a wire whisk until the mixture is bubbly and has thickened. Cook 2 minutes more. Remove from the heat and let cool a little.

3. Stir in the fruit and spoon the filling into a prebaked tart shell or tartlet shells. Serve with whipped cream or nondairy whipped topping if you like.

Makes enough to fill one 9" tart shell or six 2½" tartlet shells.

Louisa's Orange Glaze

This glaze will make a pie or tart shiny and pretty, just like the ones in delicatessens. The color of the fruit comes through, but comes through glistening. If you cook a larger batch and make it a bit thicker, it's also a good pie filling. It can even be stirred into cooked carrots.

½ cup frozen orange juice concentrate
½ cup water
½ cup sugar
2 teaspoons cornstarch, dissolved in 2 teaspoons water

1. In a medium saucepan, boil the frozen orange juice concentrate, water, and sugar until the sugar has dissolved.

2. Add the cornstarch to the boiling mixture and continue to cook until it has thickened, stirring constantly. Use in any way you wish.

Makes about 1⅓ cups.

And Other Confections

I DO HAVE A SWEET TOOTH. AND AS YOU SEE, I'M PASSING ON TO YOU MORE DESSERT and sweets recipes than other kinds. One reason is that my family, starting with my mother and aunts, has always loved entertaining, loved serving up delicious meals to company. And the icing on this entertaining is, of course, dessert. Dessert has to be perfectly wonderful. Because of this philosophy, we've collected a lot of awfully good dessert recipes. I hope you enjoy them as much as we have.

Huguenot Torte

A wonderful dessert that you can make ahead and freeze, and in Charleston Huguenots have been making it forever. The Huguenots here are French Protestants who were forced out of their country three hundred years ago. They're still holding services in French down at the Huguenot church, a beautiful place to visit.

This is a very sweet confection, so be sure to serve it with the whipped cream to balance the flavors a bit.

4 large eggs

3 cups sugar

3 tablespoons all-purpose flour

1 tablespoon baking powder

½ teaspoon salt

1 large tart apple, peeled, cored, and finely chopped (about 2 cups)

2 cups finely chopped pecans or walnuts
(pecans are more traditional)

2 teaspoons vanilla extract

½ pint heavy cream, whipped and lightly sweetened with sugar

1. Preheat the oven to 325°F and grease an 8" × 12" baking dish. Set aside.

2. Beat the eggs until they are lemon colored and frothy. Add the sugar, flour, baking powder, salt, chopped apple, chopped nuts, and vanilla extract. Mix until well combined.

3. Pour the batter into the prepared pan and bake in the preheated oven for about 45 minutes. Start peeking at it after 35 minutes. The torte will be crusty and brown when it's ready. It falls almost immediately after coming out of the oven.

4. When cool, scoop out of the baking dish with a spatula and top with the whipped cream.

Serves 8 people.

Gertie's Brown Betty

We have this often in Flat Rock, as we are usually up there during apple season. After it bakes, it still has quite a bit of liquid, but after it sits for a while, most of the liquid is absorbed.

5 medium tart, crisp apples, peeled and cored
  (save the peels and cores)
Juice of 1 lemon
1 cup light brown sugar
1 teaspoon ground cinnamon
6 slices white bread
2 tablespoons unsalted butter

BROWN SUGAR HARD SAUCE:
8 tablespoons unsalted butter, at room temperature
1 ½ cups light brown sugar
½ cup light cream
1 teaspoon vanilla extract

1. Preheat the oven to 350°F and grease a 1½-quart casserole dish. Set aside.

2. Thinly slice the apples and sprinkle them with the lemon juice and ½ cup of the brown sugar. Set aside.

3. Place the apple peels and cores in a medium saucepan, cover with water, and boil gently for 5 minutes. Remove from the heat and

with a slotted spoon remove and discard the peels and cores. Pour about 1¾ cups of the liquid from the saucepan over the apple slices. Discard any remaining liquid.

4. In a medium saucepan, bring the apple slices and liquid to a simmer and cook until you can stick a fork into the slices but they are still firm. Do not let the slices become mushy. Remove from the heat and set aside.

5. Put ½ teaspoon cinnamon in the bowl of a food processor with 3 slices of the bread. Pulse a couple of times, until you have bread crumbs. Pour out the crumbs and set aside.

6. Put the remaining ½ teaspoon cinnamon and 3 slices bread in the food-processor bowl and add the remaining ½ cup brown sugar. Process until you have bread crumbs. Set aside. This will be the Brown Betty topping.

7. Spoon half of the apples and liquid into the prepared casserole dish. Sprinkle with the first portion of bread crumbs. Spoon the remaining apples and liquid over the crumbs and then top with the second portion of bread crumbs, the ones with the brown sugar. Dot with the butter.

8. Bake uncovered in the preheated oven for 15 minutes. Reduce the oven temperature to 300°F and bake for 15 minutes more.

9. While the Brown Betty is baking, make the brown sugar hard sauce. Cream the butter and brown sugar in a medium bowl. Beat in the cream until the mixture is well combined and fluffy. Beat in the vanilla extract. Let the Brown Betty cool slightly before serving with the sauce.

Serves 6 people.

Deep-Dish Fruit Cobbler

Another of my favorite, very easy, very popular recipes is this one, which is so colorful and delicious. I find myself making it often in Flat Rock in the summer, when peaches and blueberries are plentiful.

8 tablespoons margarine, melted
1 cup self-rising flour
1 ½ cups sugar
1 cup milk
1 quart peaches, peeled, pitted, and sliced
1 pint blueberries, washed

1. Preheat the oven to 375°F.

2. Pour the melted margarine over the bottom of a deep dish 9" pie plate. Set aside.

3. In a medium bowl, thoroughly combine the flour and 1 cup of the sugar. Stir in the milk until just combined. Pour over the melted margarine in the pie plate, but *do not stir*.

4. In a large bowl, combine the peach slices and blueberries and pour over the flour-milk mixture. Again, *do not stir*.

5. Sprinkle the remaining ½ cup sugar over the fruit. Bake in the preheated oven for 40 to 45 minutes, until golden brown. Remove from the oven and cool just a bit before serving.

Serves 8 people.

Mocha Mousse

My mother adored this dessert. When we stayed at the beach in the summer she would come once a week to visit and I'd ask, "So what do you want for lunch?" She'd always say, "Stuffed crabs and mocha mousse." Oh, such a smacking of lips and praise and going on about how delicious it all was. I love this mousse myself. It must be prepared the day before you are going to serve it, though, since it needs a night to firm up in the refrigerator.

1 envelope Knox unflavored gelatin, dissolved in ¼ cup water
1 cup sugar
3 rounded tablespoons instant coffee
⅛ teaspoon salt
6 ounces semi-sweet chocolate chips
4 large eggs, separated
1 cup milk
1 teaspoon vanilla extract
1 pint heavy cream
½ teaspoon almond extract

1. In the top of a double boiler over hot water, combine the gelatin, ½ cup of the sugar, and the instant coffee, salt, chocolate chips, egg yolks, and milk. Stir constantly until the chocolate has melted and the mixture has thickened. Remove from the heat and beat briefly with an electric mixer. Stir in the vanilla extract and set aside to cool.

2. In a large bowl, beat the egg whites until they form soft peaks. Beat in ¼ cup of the sugar, 1 tablespoon at a time, until the egg whites form stiff peaks.

3. Whip ½ pint of the heavy cream and fold into the egg whites. Fold this mixture into the cooled chocolate mixture, transfer to a serving bowl or individual bowls, and refrigerate overnight.

4. Before serving, whip the remaining ½ pint heavy cream, along with the remaining ¼ cup sugar and the almond extract, until it forms soft peaks. Spoon over the mousse.

VARIATION: I often serve the mousse with ladyfingers that have been brushed or drizzled with sherry. If I want to be especially stylish, I line the serving bowl with the sherry-brushed ladyfingers before I pour the mousse into it.

Serves 6 to 8 people.

Lucille's Luscious Do-Ahead Chocolate-and-Vanilla Dessert

Lucille is an old, old friend of mine. Her mother, who was from New Orleans, was a great bridge-playing friend of my mother. And now Lucille and I are dear friends in the next generation.

2 ½ cups crushed Oreos (about 24 cookies)
8 tablespoons unsalted butter or margarine, melted
½ gallon vanilla ice cream, softened (but not melted)
14 ounces semi-sweet chocolate
⅔ cup evaporated milk
⅛ teaspoon salt
⅔ cup sugar
1 teaspoon vanilla extract

1 pint heavy cream, whipped, or 1 16-ounce container nondairy
   whipped topping
Shaved chocolate or chopped nuts for sprinkling

1. Spread the crushed Oreos over the bottom of a 9" × 13" Pyrex
   pan. Drizzle the melted butter or margarine over the cookies.
   Spread the softened ice cream over this and place in the freezer for
   about 1 hour, until firm.

2. In the top of a double boiler over hot water, combine the
   chocolate, evaporated milk, salt, sugar, and vanilla extract. Stir
   constantly for about 4 minutes. Remove from the heat and cool
   completely.

3. Remove the pie from the freezer and pour the chocolate mixture
   over the top. Put back in the freezer for at least 2 hours. Before
   serving, spread the whipped cream or nondairy whipped topping
   over the pie and then sprinkle with the shaved chocolate or nuts or
   both. Serve immediately.

Serves 12 people.

Soft, Hot Chocolate Dessert

*This dessert is company fare with the very best foot forward. It can be
served by itself or with vanilla ice cream.*

¾ cup sugar
1 cup all-purpose flour
2 teaspoons baking powder
¼ teaspoon salt
2 tablespoons vegetable shortening, chilled

3 tablespoons unsalted butter, melted
½ cup milk
1 teaspoon vanilla extract

TOPPING:
½ cup sugar
½ cup firmly packed light brown sugar
¼ cup unsweetened cocoa

1. Preheat the oven to 350°F and grease a shallow 2-quart casserole dish. Set aside.

2. Sift together the sugar, flour, baking powder, and salt. Cut in the vegetable shortening. Set aside.

3. In a small bowl, mix together the melted butter, milk, and vanilla extract. Add this mixture to the flour mixture and combine thoroughly. Spread in the prepared casserole dish.

4. In a medium bowl, mix together the ingredients for the topping. Sprinkle over the batter. Pour 1½ cups water over everything in the casserole dish. DO NOT STIR. Bake uncovered in the preheated oven for 35 to 40 minutes. Serve immediately.

Serve 6 to 8 people.

Custard Made in a Double Boiler

This custard takes only about ten minutes from start to finish, not including chilling time. If you cook it too long, it will curdle. Experience is the best teacher when it comes to making a perfect custard.

2 cups milk
2 whole eggs plus 2 additional egg yolks

⅓ cup sugar
¼ teaspoon salt
½ tablespoon all-purpose flour
2 teaspoons vanilla extract

1. In a medium saucepan, scald the milk. Remove from the heat.

2. With an electric mixer, beat the eggs, additional egg yolks, sugar, salt, and flour until the mixture is a lemon color. Pour the scalded milk into the mixture but do not beat. Pour the mixture into the top of a double boiler over boiling water. Stir constantly until the mixture is thick enough to coat a wooden spoon. Do not allow the custard to boil. Remove from the heat and stir in the vanilla extract.

3. Pour the custard into 6 to 8 small ramekins. Chill thoroughly before serving.

Serves 6 to 8 people.

Crème Brûlée

This is a perfectly delicious dessert—one of the world's favorites and consistently the favorite of all the men in my life. It is a baked custard topped with a crunchy caramel crust. Brûlée means "burnt." The custard may be made a couple of days ahead and kept in the refrigerator. Making it at least a day ahead ensures that it will be thoroughly chilled when it comes time to make the caramelized crust. Do not freeze this custard— or any custard.

8 egg yolks
1 quart heavy cream

1 tablespoon vanilla extract
4 tablespoons sugar
Pinch of salt
1 cup light brown sugar

1. Preheat the oven to 350°F.

2. With an electric mixer, beat the egg yolks until they are a light
   lemon color. Set aside.

3. In a large saucepan, scald the cream, vanilla extract, sugar, and
   salt. Stir until the sugar is completely dissolved. Pour in the
   beaten egg yolks and combine thoroughly. Remove from the heat
   and strain the mixture into a large bowl. Transfer to a shallow 10"
   baking dish or to eight 4-ounce ramekins. Place the baking dish or
   ramekins in a pan of hot water. The water should come about
   three-quarters of the way up the sides of the baking dish or
   ramekins. Bake in the preheated oven for 40 to 50 minutes, until a
   knife inserted in the center comes out almost clean. The custard
   will continue to cook for a few minutes as it cools. When it is
   absolutely, completely cooled, put it in the refrigerator. Chill for
   at least a day.

4. To prepare the caramelized crust, press the brown sugar through a
   sieve over the custard. Gently spread over the custard, creating a
   layer about ⅛" thick. The brown sugar must be as evenly spread as
   possible. Place 4 to 6 inches under the broiler for about a minute,
   until the brown sugar bubbles and becomes caramelized. Do not
   leave your broiler unattended. It's easy to burn the sugar, but don't
   panic if you do. Just lift off the scorched brown sugar with a thin
   spatula and start over.

5. Let the custard sit for 10 minutes after it comes out of the oven, until the crust is brittle. Put it back in the refrigerator and serve in 1 to 3 hours.

Serves 8 people.

Crème Caramel

A classic. I'm willing to bet you there's more custard ordered in restaurants than any other kind of dessert. Custards are a clear favorite among men.

1 cup sugar
2 teaspoons water
2 cups milk
1 cup light cream
Zest of 2 lemons
3 whole eggs plus 3 additional egg yolks, lightly beaten
¼ teaspoon salt

1. Preheat the oven to 325°F.

2. In a heavy skillet over medium heat, combine ½ cup of the sugar and the water, shaking the pan occasionally until the mixture boils and forms a light amber syrup. Stir to blend and cook a few seconds more. Do not overcook or the caramel will have a bitter taste. Pour at once into a straight-sided, ovenproof 1-quart mold and turn the mold to coat the bottom and sides. Set aside.

3. In a heavy saucepan over very low heat, warm the milk and cream with the lemon zest until a film forms on the top. Remove from the heat.

4. In a large bowl, thoroughly combine the eggs and additional egg yolks, salt, and remaining ½ cup sugar. Gradually pour the hot milk-cream mixture into the egg mixture, stirring constantly with a wire whisk.

5. Pour the mixture slowly into the caramel-lined mold, being careful to avoid creating bubbles. Place the mold in a pan of lukewarm water and bake in the preheated oven for 45 to 60 minutes, until a knife inserted in the center comes out almost clean. The pan of water should never boil during baking; if it begins to boil, add some cold water to the pan. When the custard has finished baking, let it cool to room temperature, then chill in the refrigerator for at least several hours, but preferably overnight. To remove from the mold, gently loosen the edges with the tip of a sharp knife, then place a serving plate over the mold and turn it over.

Serves 6 people.

Laura's Coffee Jelly

I had this once at my friend Laura's and thought it delicious and different, but of course I'm fond of all jellies.

2 envelopes Knox unflavored gelatin
½ cup cold water
1 cup boiling water
1½ tablespoons sugar
2 cups strong coffee
½ teaspoon vanilla extract

MACAROON CREAM:

1½ cups heavy cream

3 tablespoons sugar

1 jigger good rum

1 cup crumbled almond macaroons

1. Dissolve the gelatin in the cold water. Add the boiling water and sugar and stir well. Allow to cool for 20 minutes.

2. Add the coffee and vanilla extract and stir well. Pour into a 9" ring mold coated with vegetable oil cooking spray. Chill in the refrigerator for 5 hours.

3. Just before serving, make the macaroon cream. Whip the heavy cream until it forms soft peaks. Fold in the sugar, rum, and crumbled macaroons. Carefully unmold the coffee jelly onto a pretty plate and fill the center with the macaroon cream. Serve immediately.

Serves 6 people.

Orange-Banana Sherbet

My children love this. Very cooling. I wish I had an acre of bananas in my backyard. They do grow here, but they look pretty messy when the cold knocks them back. Anyway, the banana freighters unload at our docks, so we have an unending supply.

1 12-ounce can frozen orange juice concentrate

1 tablespoon fresh lemon juice

1 cup sugar

1½ cups water

1 cup ice water

1½ cups mashed ripe banana (about 3 bananas)

1. Put the frozen orange juice concentrate and lemon juice in a large bowl.

2. In a medium saucepan, bring the sugar and 1½ cups water to a boil, stirring regularly. Pour over the orange juice concentrate and lemon juice. When the concentrate has melted, pour in the ice water and stir until well combined. Stir the banana into the orange mixture and combine thoroughly.

3. Pour the mixture into a loaf pan or other container and place in the freezer. Stir several times while the sherbet is freezing. It should be ready to serve in about 3 hours.

Serves 8 to 10 people.

Index